The Capital Ring

The Capital Ring

Colin Saunders

Aurum
Press

Quarto is the authority on a wide range of topics.
Quarto educates, entertains and enriches the lives of
our readers – enthusiasts and lovers of hands-on living.
www.QuartoKnows.com

Acknowledgements

The Capital Ring owes its existence to the imagination and hard work of many people. The idea was Roger Warhurst's, and Brian Bellwood led a team of researchers who walked out the proposed route. Jim Walker, Stuart McLeod and the Orbitals Working Party of the London Walking Forum co-ordinated discussions with the London boroughs, and an army of officers from the London boroughs helped with finalising the route, providing details for this book and organising signage. Many other individuals and organisations have contributed information. The author is especially grateful to the late David Sharp, chairman of the Orbitals Working Party, for providing most of the photographs and checking the route description; to Jenny Knight, former Capital Ring Route Manager; to Alexandra Rook and Abi Mansley, formerly of Walk London; to Lisa Tozer of Walk England; and to Spencer Clark and others at Transport for London.

This revised and updated edition published in 2016 by Aurum Press Limited
74–77 White Lion Street, London N1 9PF • www.aurumpress.co.uk
First published in 2003

Text copyright © Colin Saunders 2003, 2006, 2008, 2010, 2012, 2014, 2016

Photographs copyright © David Sharp 2003: 12, 15, 24–5, 30, 38, 44, 46, 54, 56, 62, 68–9, 70, 72, 74, 76, 82, 86–7, 92, 96, 105, 106, 120, 130–1, 138, 140–1, 148, 154–5; Colin Saunders 2010, 2012: 16, 21, 26, 33, 35, 42, 48, 81, 88, 103, 112, 115, 125, 128, 132, 135, 136, 146, 156, 158; Alamy 2012: 1, 2–3, 10–11, 18–19, 60, 84, 118; Mike Waite 2012: 98, 110; Nigel Reeve 2012: 41

This product includes mapping data licensed from Ordnance Survey® with the permission of the Controller of Her Majesty's Stationery Office. © Crown copyright 2016.
All rights reserved. Licence number 43453U.

Ordnance Survey and Travelmaster are registered trademarks and the Ordnance Survey symbol and Explorer are trademarks of Ordnance Survey, the national mapping agency of Great Britain.

ISBN 978 1 78131 569 9

Book design by Robert Updegraff • Printed and bound in China

Cover photograph: *The ArcelorMittal Orbit (Walk 14)*
Half-title photograph: *A grandstand view of the Olympic Stadium from The Greenway (Walk 14)*
Title-page photograph: *Syon House (Walk 7) is the London home of the Duke and Duchess of Northumberland*

Aurum Press want to ensure that these Trail Guides are always as up to date as possible – but stiles collapse, pubs close and bus services change all the time. If, on walking this path, you discover any important changes of which future walkers need to be aware, do let us know. Either email us on **trailguides@aurumpress.co.uk** with your comments, or if you take the trouble to drop us a line to:
Trail Guides, Aurum Press, 74–77 White Lion Street, London N1 9PF,
we'll send you a free guide of your choice as thanks.

Contents

Distance checklist

		Distances (excluding links)	
		miles	**km**
1	Woolwich to Falconwood	6.2	10.0
2	Falconwood to Grove Park	3.5	5.6
3	Grove Park to Crystal Palace	7.7	12.4
4	Crystal Palace to Streatham	4.1	6.6
5	Streatham to Wimbledon Park	5.5	8.8
6	Wimbledon Park to Richmond	7.0	11.3
7	Richmond to Osterley Lock	4.0	6.4
8	Osterley Lock to Greenford	4.9	7.9
9	Greenford to South Kenton	5.5	8.8
10	South Kenton to Hendon Park	6.2	10.0
11	Hendon Park to Highgate	5.3	8.5
12	Highgate to Stoke Newington	5.4	8.5
13	Stoke Newington to Hackney Wick	3.7	6.0
14	Hackney Wick to Beckton District Park	4.9	7.9
15	Beckton District Park to Woolwich	3.7	6.0

How to use this guide

The format of this book is similar to that of its companion, *The London Loop* by David Sharp, also published by Aurum. The introduction sets out background and general information, which should set the scene and help you understand how the route was conceived and planned. It tells you something about the London Walking Forum, without which the route would never have got up and running, and Transport for London (TfL), which now promotes London's Strategic Walks. It goes on to describe the route in general, the signs, and the plentiful public transport opportunities. There is some advice on walking safely, and on how accessible the route is for people using wheelchairs and buggies. Finally, the introduction puts in perspective the historical background to the area covered by the Capital Ring.

Next, the Capital Ring is described in detail, divided into the 15 consecutive walks that were planned jointly by the London Walking Forum and relevant London boroughs. At the start of each chapter, the route of the Capital Ring is shown in outline, with a white arrow (shown right) indicating the start point of the section. On each walk there are official Capital Ring links with nearby stations, and these too are described. The route is marked on maps prepared specially by the Ordnance Survey® from their 1:25 000 Explorer™ maps, enlarged to 1:16 666 to show the route more clearly. With text and maps on facing pages, you should find it easy to follow the Capital Ring, especially now that the route has been fully signed and waymarked. Letters are used to identify key points along the route, both in the text and on the maps. Special features of interest are numbered in the same way. Pubs, cafés, toilets, museums and car parks on or very near the route are identified by their individual logos on the maps. The total distances for each walk and the station links are shown to the nearest decimal point in miles and kilometres, elsewhere in miles and yards only. Station links and other diversions are shown in italics, to distinguish them from the main route description. *Some maps start on a right-hand page and continue on the left-hand page – black arrows (➞) at the edge of the maps indicate the start point.*

The final section contains more information about public transport, useful addresses, including the borough councils that are responsible for installation and maintenance of the signs and waymarks, and a list of the Ordnance Survey® maps that cover the route.

David Sharp

Sadly, David Sharp died in April 2015. As well as providing most of the photographs for this guide, as chairman of the Orbitals Working Party of the London Walking Forum he steered the development and promotion of the Capital Ring and London Loop, and the author is most grateful to David for all his help and encouragement in writing this guide.

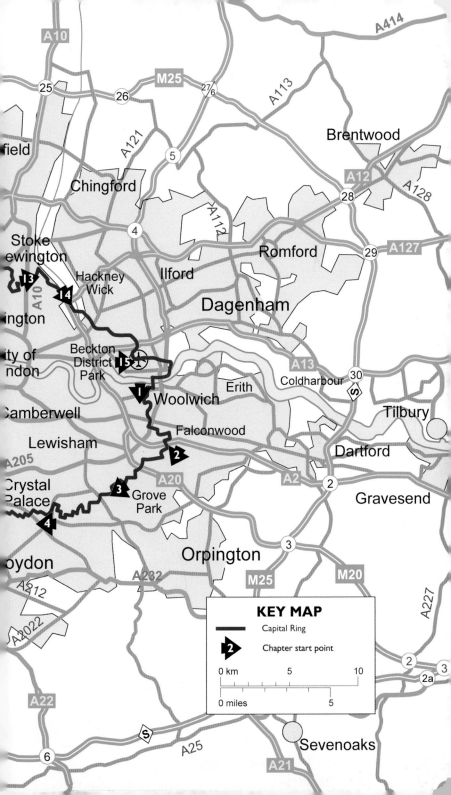

KEY MAP

—— Capital Ring

◢2 Chapter start point

0 km   5   10

0 miles   5

Dappled fallow deer and the larger red
deer roam freely in Richmond Park (Walk
6). Do not approach the antlered males –
they can be dangerous!

PART ONE
Introduction

Near the derelict chapel, Dr Isaac Watts gazes across Abney Park Cemetery in Stoke Newington, now a nature reserve (Walk 12).

Approaching London from the air, passengers are often struck by the abundance of greenery that permeates the urban sprawl. Those green spaces may not be so easily found on the ground, but this book will guide you through at least 50 of them along the Capital Ring, a walking route of 78 miles (125 km) that is easily divided into bite-sized chunks. The green spaces are linked by stretches beside water and along pleasant residential roads, and you will pass many points of interest.

The Capital Ring forms an inner circle for walkers around Greater London, while its big brother, the 150-mile (241-km) London Loop, provides the outer circle. Both routes are now part of Transport for London's strategic walk network. The Ring lies between 4 and 10 miles (6.4 and 16 km) from Charing Cross, on average about three-quarters of the way from central London to the Greater London boundary, while the Loop closely follows the boundary itself. In Travelcard terms, the Capital Ring meanders mostly through Zones 3 and 4, occasionally straying into Zone 2.

You will see some of London's outstanding attractions, such as the Thames Barrier, Eltham Palace, and Wimbledon Common with its windmill. You will have a grandstand view of the Olympic Stadium, constructed for the London Olympics and Paralympics in 2012. The route passes nearly 200 historic 'listed buildings', which are protected by law from destruction or unsuitable development. And you pass by or through many nature reserves, including Richmond Park, where you can spot herds of deer, while Syon Park is virtually a theme park. There is waterside walking aplenty on the Thames and its tributaries, the Grand Union Canal, Brent Reservoir (Welsh Harp), the Lee Navigation and in Docklands. Green areas of all sizes along the route include parks, woods and even occasional pastures. You will come across some little-known gems, such as Oxleas Meadows, the Parkland Walk, Abney Park Cemetery, The Greenway and the Docklands Campus of the University of East London.

There are breathtaking views right from the start at Woolwich, where a vista along the River Thames includes the Thames Barrier, Canary Wharf and the O$_2$ Arena (formerly the Millennium Dome). From sea level at the outset, the route rises to several comparatively high points in London terms, reaching altitudes of around 300–400 feet (90–120 metres) with extensive panoramas. The Thames is a dominant feature of the route, encountered three times. Although it is nearly a quarter of a mile (half a kilometre) wide at Woolwich, this does not prevent you from completing the circle on foot, as it is possible to cross underwater through a foot tunnel.

Walk London

The Walk London Network was set up in 2005 (as the Strategic Walk Network) by Transport for London (TfL) and comprises seven high-quality walking routes that span the capital. They include the two Orbital Walks (Capital Ring and London Loop), Green Chain Walk, Jubilee Greenway, Jubilee Walkway and Lea Valley Walk, plus the Thames Path within Greater London. Information sheets for all these routes are free to download from the TfL website: www.tfl.gov.uk/walking.

The ambitious proposal for the London Orbital Walks was first suggested in 1990 by the London Walking Forum, predecessor to Walk London, and the Forum's Orbitals Working Party then set about making it happen in partnership with the London boroughs through which the routes pass. Transport for London provided £9 million of funding between 2005 and 2012 to raise all the routes to a consistently high standard. The routes continue to be promoted by TfL and its partners through regular events such as the popular and free led-walk weekends, held three times each year.

Walking the Capital Ring

The Capital Ring is divided into 15 separate walks, ranging from 3.5 to 7.7 miles (5.6 to 12.4 km) and averaging just over 5 miles (8 km). To cover the whole route, the logical starting place is of course the beginning of Walk 1, on the south side of the Woolwich Foot Tunnel. But there is no compulsion to follow the sections in progressive order; you can join and leave at any convenient point in any order. As the route is described clockwise here, it may be easier to go in this direction; but signage was completed in 2005 so it should be possible to follow the route in either direction as preferred. If walking in the early morning or late evening, or on Christmas Day, bear in mind that some of the smaller parks along the route may be closed – times can be checked with the parks department of the relevant London borough (see Useful Addresses, page 163).

Route changes. There are times when parts of the Capital Ring may have to be diverted from the route described in this book, in which case an alternative route should be signposted.

Signs and waymarks

A variety of signs and waymarks indicate the route on the ground. In open spaces these consist mostly of a simple white disc, mounted on wooden posts and containing a directional arrow with the Big Ben logo in blue and text in green. A word of warning: the arrow's direction may not be clear until you are close up. It is easy to assume that it points ahead, but it may indicate a turn – look closely before continuing.

On streets, the posts are replaced by larger aluminium signs strapped to lampposts and other street furniture, and these additionally carry a walking-man symbol. They carry the logo on a green background – but note that in the London Boroughs of Richmond and Harrow, black replaces green due to local conservation area considerations. At major focal points you will also encounter tall main signs that give distances to three or four points in either direction. The link routes with stations have all been signed, and on these the word 'link' is incorporated into the Capital Ring logo.

It is possible that some signs or waymarks may have been affected or removed by vandalism or accidental damage. When in doubt, it will probably be best to stick to the route description in this book. If you come across such instances, it would be appreciated if you could report them. This can be done by contacting the relevant borough council (as indicated in the text and in Useful Addresses, page 163).

The magnificently carved front door of Charlton House, one of the best examples of a Jacobean building in London (Walk 1).

Reaching the Capital Ring

The route is designed to pass by or close to stations, and walkers should find using public transport most convenient. In fact, the route passes or has links to 47 stations, and there are many bus routes in between. Most lie within Travelcard Zones 2, 3 and 4 – just one (Harrow-on-the-Hill) is in Zone 5. For further details, see the Transport section on page 161.

Although some hardy souls in the Long Distance Walkers Association have walked the whole Capital Ring in one go, most people will choose to take it in easy stages, so that the route will become a

A typical Capital Ring aluminium street sign, showing the walking-man symbol and the Big Ben logo.

series of linear walks. For most Londoners, this will involve travelling out and back from home each time. Visitors are also likely to find it more practical to base themselves in reasonably central accommodation, travelling as above, rather than moving to new lodgings each night, though this may be possible if preferred.

Safety first

The route has been designed to minimise road walking, but inevitably much of it follows or crosses some busy roads – in this book they can be identified by an 'A' or 'B' followed by a number. When crossing any road, common sense should of course prevail: you should only cross when it is safe to do so. Where possible, the route uses controlled or protected crossings, but there are a few places where a short diversion to a controlled crossing is advisable – attention is drawn to these in the route description. There are just a couple of spots where no crossing is available and extra care is therefore needed.

The Capital Ring main sign at Ballot Box Bridge (Walk 9).

The description suggests which side of the road to follow where this helps you to cross an approaching major road at a protected point, or reduces the number of road crossings. The route goes through a few golf courses, where you should watch out for stray flying golf balls, especially when crossing a fairway. Always allow golfers to finish their stroke if your passing might disturb their concentration.

Much of the route follows 'shared paths', which are used by both pedestrians and cyclists. Some of them have been specially prepared to provide separate lanes for each class of user, but others have no demarcation. Regrettably, some cyclists irresponsibly use paths or pavements that are only intended for pedestrians, so you should always be alert for the possibility that a cyclist may approach from behind without warning.

Accessibility

Much of the route should be accessible to people using wheelchairs or buggies, but what may or may not be accessible will depend on individual circumstances. As a guide, Walks 4, 5, 7, 11, 13, 14 and 15 are mostly on a firm, level surface, though there are some exceptions. The other walks include some stretches that may be accessible. Elsewhere, steps, steep gradients, grass or uneven surfaces may make progress difficult or impossible. Where a practical alternative has been identified, this is also described. For each walk there is a general description under the heading 'Surface and terrain', which, together with the route description, should enable readers to judge its suitability.

Points of interest

The author has tried to identify as many points of interest along the route as possible, but due to limitations of space it has not been practical to delve too deeply. Much of the history is common to the whole area. Prior to the Roman period, it was populated by Celtic tribes, most of whom knuckled under and became Romanised, building villas and settlements close to roads out of London. If it had been invented before the formation of the County of London in 1888 and that of Greater London in 1965, the Capital Ring would have passed through the counties of Kent, Surrey, Middlesex and Essex, dating from Saxon times. Most of the towns and villages have names that are modified versions of the original Saxon settlements, established between the eighth century AD and the Norman Conquest in 1066.

The coming of the railways during the 19th century greatly affected the whole area, leading to a massive migration to more comfortable dwellings in what would henceforth be known as 'the suburbs' or 'the commuter belt'. It is to the everlasting credit of more enlightened citizens at that time that so much open space was saved from housing development for the walkers of today. Most of the parks and open spaces you pass through are owned by the appropriate London borough, though there are some exceptions, to which attention is drawn in the text.

There are pubs, cafés and toilets at frequent intervals on or close to most of the route. However, you should be prepared for some long gaps, particularly on Walks 10 and 14.

The gates of the Thames Barrier (Walk 1) normally lie on the river bed, but in times of flood danger, or for testing, they can be raised or lowered in 45 minutes.

PART TWO
The Capital Ring

1 Woolwich to Falconwood

Distance 6.2 miles (10 km). Excludes Capital Ring links at each end: Woolwich Arsenal 0.8 miles (1.3 km); Falconwood 0.3 miles (0.5 km).

Public transport The start of Walk 1 is 200 yards from bus stops in Hare Street. It is around a quarter of a mile from Royal Arsenal Pier, three-quarters of a mile from Woolwich Arsenal Station and more buses in General Gordon Place, and half a mile from North Woolwich Bus Station via the Woolwich Foot Tunnel or Woolwich Free Ferry. There is a link from Woolwich Dockyard Station. The finish is about 500 yards from Falconwood Station and bus stops. All stations on this walk are in Travelcard Zone 4, except Woolwich Dockyard and Charlton, which are in Zone 3.

Surface and terrain Woolwich to Woolwich Road: level paving or tarmac with some short, gentle slopes and two flights of steps

(alternative ramp nearby). Woolwich Road to Charlton Park Road: on paving or tarmac but with some fairly steep ascents and descents; includes one very long upward flight of steps, which can be avoided along a signed diversion. Charlton Park Road to Shooters Hill: mostly level paving or tarmac but some grass and earth paths with gentle descents across Woolwich Common. Shooters Hill to Falconwood: mostly uneven paths and tracks, which may be muddy in places, with some long and fairly steep ascents and one long downward flight of steps (with signed avoiding diversion)

Refreshments Woolwich, Woolwich Road, Charlton Park, Shooters Hill, Severndroog Castle, Oxleas Meadows and Falconwood.

Toilets Woolwich, Maryon Park, Charlton Park, Severndroog Castle and Oxleas Meadows.

Capital Ring link from Woolwich Arsenal Stations, Royal Arsenal Pier and bus stops (0.8 miles/1.3 km). *From the station exits* **A**, *turn right along Woolwich New Road. Go over the zebra crossing then keep ahead into the market place. Bear right past the Royal Arsenal gatehouse (toilets on your left) then cross the dual carriageway Beresford Street* **B**. *Keep ahead into the Royal Arsenal Riverside complex along the broad pedestrianised No. 1 Street, which swings right as it passes between the Gate House and Dial Arch pubs* **C**, *then passes the Firepower Museum. On reaching Royal Arsenal Pier* **D** *turn left beside the River Thames and follow the riverside walk for a quarter of a mile to a slipway (toilets). Keep ahead between the river and the Waterfront Leisure Centre to the circular, red-brick structure that forms the exit from the Woolwich Foot Tunnel* **E**.

If you prefer to travel to North Woolwich **F**, *from the bus station head for the circular brick building and go through the Woolwich Foot Tunnel (see Walk 15), or you can use the*

The history of Woolwich can be traced back to pre-Roman times, with evidence of an Iron Age (Celtic) settlement near the present ferry terminal. The Romans occupied a fortified encampment in the hills to the west, then the Saxons returned to the riverside to establish a fishing village, with the strange spelling Uuluuich (probably meaning 'wool harbour'); this was before the existence of the letter W. The Royal Naval Dockyard in 1512 was the first of several major institutions to be established here, the others being the Royal Arsenal (1545), the Royal Military Academy (1721) and the Woolwich Equitable Building Society ('The Woolwich', 1847). All have now closed or moved away, though the building society still has several

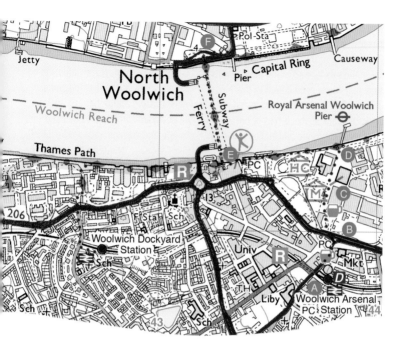

branches in the area. In 1886, workers at the Royal Arsenal formed a football club known first as Dial Square, then Royal Arsenal, then Woolwich Arsenal, and finally plain Arsenal, but in 1913 it too moved away, to Highbury, North London.

Walk 1 of the Capital Ring starts beside the River Thames, at the south end of the Woolwich Foot Tunnel **E**, from which you should emerge triumphantly 78 miles (125 km) later on completing the route. The whole of Walk 1 keeps within the Royal Borough of Greenwich. By the tunnel exit, you will find the first of the Capital Ring's main signposts. Other folk dressed for walking around here may not be following the Capital Ring: the post also carries the signs of the south-east extension of the Thames Path, denoted by a sailing barge logo,

The Woolwich Ferry has connected communities north and south of the Thames since the 12th century.

and the distinctive plaques of the Jubilee Greenway are set in the ground. The Capital Ring shares its route with both these trails as far as Maryon Park, and its logo has simply been added to the Thames Path signs. You must watch out for cyclists too, as this is part of the Thames Cycle Route and National Cycle Route 1.

With your back to the tunnel building and facing the river, go left along the brick roadway, bear left and then right, under a bridge, around the back of some buildings. A short slope leads up to the Ferry Approach Road. Cross with care then turn right down the far side of the approach to the Woolwich Free Ferry **1**. It is likely that a ferry has existed here since the late 12th century. A toll was charged until 1889, but pressure from the people of Woolwich resulted in its being dropped and the service has since been free, financed by various incarnations of the governing authority for London.

At the blue ferry control cabin **F**, turn left beside a car park and snack bar. To your left rises the tower of the 18th-century St Mary Magdalene Church. This area was for four centuries the Royal Naval Dockyard **2**, established in 1512 when the *Great Harry* was built here – King Henry VIII's flagship and the biggest warship of its time. The dockyard expanded and many other famous ships were launched here,

Woolwich

The ancient town of Woolwich has an incredibly rich history, having once been the home of the army, the navy, the Royal Arsenal Co-operative Society, Arsenal Football Club and, of course, 'The Woolwich' itself – the Woolwich Equitable Building Society. All have now departed, but the land they vacated has been put to good use.

including HMS *Beagle*, which from 1831 took five years to circumnavigate the globe with Charles Darwin on board as naturalist. Naval shipbuilding gradually moved to other locations, finally ceasing altogether in 1869, but the dockyard continued to be used for storage and administration until 1926, when it was sold to the Royal Arsenal Co-operative Society for warehousing. The land remained classified as secret, and depiction of the layout on maps was prohibited until fairly recently.

Continue along the riverside, here known as Woolwich Dockyard Promenade. A splendid vista ahead encompasses in one line the Thames Barrier, the O2 Dome, Canary Wharf and of course the Thames itself, while opposite is the Tate & Lyle sugar refinery in Silvertown. You pass two former slipways and two former dry docks **G** of the Royal Naval Dockyard, also known as graving or draw docks, built in the mid-19th century. The dry docks are now stocked with fish for angling. Keep your eyes on the ground to see a rather battered, circular mosaic based on the signs of the zodiac. It was installed in 1984 by the National Elfrieda Rathbone Society, nowadays known as plain Rathbone, which helps people whose needs have not been met by education. Elfrieda Rathbone (1871–1940) was a member of an English family that fought injustice for

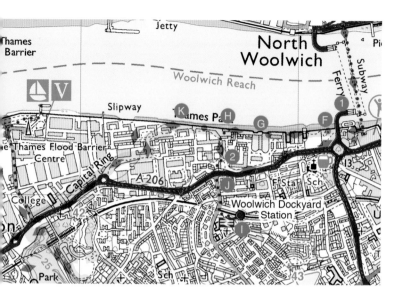

over 250 years. As a teacher at a special kindergarten for children considered 'incapable of learning', she was the inspiration behind the society's formation. A little further on, two unemployed cannon pointing harmlessly across the river are remnants of the Gun Drill Battery **H** of the same era, used for training. To the left rises the Clockhouse of 1784, once the house and office of the Dockyard Admiral-Superintendent, now a community centre.

You come to a wall, part of the flood defences, which cannot be breached, so you must either climb over the steep steps – 18 up, 11 down – or use a ramp to the left. The steps form a graceful, white cantilevered structure, known as the Linkbridge **K**, constructed in 2000 for Sustrans, the charity responsible for developing the National Cycle Network. The bridge doubles as a viewing platform, from which you have a fine view of the Thames Barrier ahead. Any river in flood can pose huge problems for those who live and work nearby, but with the Thames the dangers are magnified out of all proportion by the huge amount of extra tidal water that surges upriver at certain times. This fact was driven home in 1953, when a particularly disastrous flood drowned over 300 people and caused immense damage. The eventual

> ***Capital Ring link from Woolwich Dockyard Station*** *(0.3 miles/0.5 km). From the main exit **I**, turn right along Belson Road, then turn again down Frances Street. Cross Woolwich Church Street **J** at the traffic lights then keep ahead through the gateway into Boneta Road. Bear right, then immediately turn left along Defiance Walk, past the Clockhouse, and at the end climb the steps or ramp over the river wall to the Gun Drill Battery **H** beside the River Thames. You join the Capital Ring by turning left along the riverside.*

The view from Woolwich Dockyard Promenade encapsulates modern London in a line:the Thames Barrier, O2 Arena (formerly the Millennium Dome) and Canary Wharf.

The graceful Linkbridge provides access over a flood defence wall and doubles as a viewing platform.

result was the construction of the Thames Flood Barrier **3**, popularly known as the Thames Barrier, completed in 1984. The gates normally rest on the river bed, but in times of flood danger, or for testing, they are swung by electro-hydraulic power into an upright position between the piers; full closure of the barrier can be achieved in around 45 minutes.

In 75 yards after the Linkbridge **K** you must leave the riverside walk as it comes to a temporary end at a wall ahead. Beyond it lies the site of the great Siemens factory, where submarine cables were made from 1863 until 1968. Access through this area awaits redevelopment, so meanwhile you must leave the river, following signposts marked 'Thames Path Interim Route'.

You are now walking through the Henry's Wharf Estate, occupying the site of the Royal Naval Dockyard's Steam Factory, developed during the 1830s–1840s to build and maintain

steam engines. The tall chimney over to the left is its most visible remnant, standing 200 feet (60 metres) high. Go left then right around a red-brick apartment block and in 120 yards turn left along Ruston Road **L**. At the T-junction turn right, still in Ruston Road, past some commercial units, then bear left to the traffic roundabout **M**, with a McDonald's opposite. Cross Warspite Road and continue beside the dual carriageway A206 Woolwich Road. As you pass a set of pedestrian lights, opposite is the White Horse pub, while to your right is the green, copper-turreted Windrush Primary School, formerly Maryon Park School, built in 1896, and the brand-new Royal Greenwich University Technical College, which opened in 2013. Keep on to the next set of pedestrian lights, just before a Thames Barrier signboard **N**.

> **Capital Ring link with Thames Barrier and pier** (0.4 miles / 0.7 km). There is an optional diversion here to see at close quarters the Thames Barrier, where there are a café (sometimes closed for private functions) and toilets in the Visitor Centre **O**. To reach it, turn right immediately before the Thames Barrier board, following Green Chain Walk signs on a winding path through a narrow park. Return by the same route, following the Green Chain Walk signs to Woolwich Road and cross over to Maryon Park.

Cross at the lights by the Thames Barrier board **N** and go ahead through the gate into Maryon Park **4**. The Capital Ring now parts company with the Thames Path and Jubilee Greenway and heads south and south-west with

the Green Chain Walk (GCW) for the next 16 miles (26 km) to Crystal Palace Park. This wedge-shaped network, extending over 40 miles (64 km) through south-east London, links many woods, commons and other open spaces. Signs on this part of the Capital Ring show the logos of both routes, including the distinctive linked G-C logo. The GCW 'house colour' is also green, but a darker shade than the Capital Ring's.

Maryon Park and Maryon Wilson Park, which follows, take their name from the Maryon Wilson family, who lived at Charlton House. Both parks were part of Hanging Wood, which included a number of sandpits, the source of sand used as floor covering in the days before carpets became widely

available. In one of the pits, some 500 yards to the right of the Capital Ring, is Charlton Athletic Football Club's ground, The Valley. The mostly landscaped Maryon Park was formed from another of the pits, donated by the Maryon Wilsons to London County Council in 1891. If you have seen Michelangelo Antonioni's 1966 movie *Blow-Up*, you may recognise this as the main location.

Ignoring the GCW alternative route to the right, turn left up the slope, then right at the top. Go past the playground and cross the railway line. At a path junction **P** the Capital Ring bears right to keep the tennis courts to your left. A very long flight of steps lies ahead. *They can be avoided by following the signed GCW diversion to the left here,*

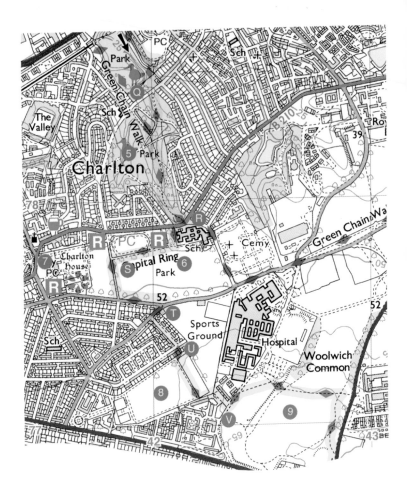

rejoining the route in Thorntree Road **Q** *below.* In 200 yards take your time as you climb the 115 steps up to your right. *There are toilets 100 yards to the left from the foot of the steps.* At the top, go through a gate then bear right on a gravel path to Thorntree Road **Q** *(buses)*, and cross into Maryon Wilson Park **5**.

You descend quite steeply on tarmac paths, with two shallow steps, to pass between the pens of a children's zoo. Turn left and climb steadily up a pretty combe beside a winding little stream to emerge at Charlton Park Road **R**, opposite Charlton Park Academy. Turn right and cross the road at the pedestrian refuge, then in a few yards turn left into Charlton Park itself **6**. Walk along the drive, past a small car park and a barrier. Turn right along a tarmac path lined with lime trees, passing a playground with a refreshment kiosk. Coming into view now is Charlton House **7** acknowledged as one of the best examples of a Jacobean building in London. It was completed in 1612 for Sir Adam Newton, tutor to Prince Henry, son of King James I. What are now known as Charlton Park, Maryon Park, Maryon Wilson Park and Hornfair Park were all part of the Charlton House estate. The house is now used as a community centre and library with a café and toilets. The area between the house and its gates used to be the village green, where the Charlton Horn Fair took place from its origin in the 16th century until 1829, when the Maryon Wilsons enclosed the green. The fair continued on a nearby field, but was banned in 1875 following increasingly drunken and libidinous behaviour. It was revived in 1973, on the original site by the house and now takes place annually again, though the time of year has varied.

On reaching a T-junction **S**, you turn left to continue along the Capital Ring. *There are toilets (in the pavilion) and a café over to your right. If you wish to visit Charlton House (which has a café and toilets), turn right then left, past the café. For pubs in Charlton village, leave the park through the gate then turn left along Charlton Park Road.*

Follow the path, now with Charlton House away to your right. On the far side of the first field (a cricket pitch in summer), a low fence indicates the presence of a ha-ha or sunken wall, intended to separate the house from the park without spoiling the view. Just before the road, turn left through a gap in the fence onto grass inside and parallel to the park fence – you can avoid the grass by walking along the pavement outside the park. In just over 200 yards leave the park through a small gate on to Charlton Park Lane.

Cross the road beside a mini-roundabout **T** at the junction with Canberra Road. Turn right then in 75 yards left along Inigo Jones Road, whose name marks a connection at Charlton House with the celebrated 17th-century architect. This leads ahead across Prince Henry Road **U** and along an alleyway into the rather bland Hornfair Park **8**. Originally known as Charlton Playing Fields, it was renamed in 1948 to commemorate the Horn Fair described above. Turn right then left along tarmac paths past a BMX track, heading for a long, red-brick building. At the end, turn left along a narrow, earth path. Go through a gap in a fence, then bear right to Baker Road **V** *(buses)*. Turn left and in 75 yards, just before the Queen Elizabeth Hospital in Stadium Road, go over a zebra crossing. Keep ahead between some iron bollards, then bear left along a grass path, diagonal to the road. This leads to a narrow tarmac path, which you follow across Woolwich Common **9**.

During the 18th and 19th centuries, Woolwich Common was sometimes a scene of mass military activity. Before engaging in an overseas campaign, the British army would assemble and camp here before going to Woolwich Arsenal to collect their weaponry and embark on ships moored in the Thames. Behind the trees to your left is the site of Woolwich Stadium, from 1920 to 1973 the scene of many military sporting engagements. Beyond that lies the Royal Artillery Barracks, which was the site of a temporary stadium for the shooting events of the Olympic and Paralympic Games in 2012. With Shooters Hill rising beyond the trees ahead, continue to a path, junction **W**. Beyond the trees lies the former Royal Military Academy **10**. Known to its graduates as 'The Shop', the academy was the precursor to the current one at Sandhurst, and replaced a much smaller one in the Royal Arsenal.

Turn right along a grassy track beside the trees, then in 200 yards fork left onto Academy Road. Turn right beside the road to the traffic lights at Shooters Hill **X** *(buses)*. Cross left at the lights over Academy Road, then right over Shooters Hill towards a red-brick building, which was a police station until 2005 but is now residential. Stretching down the hill is the grey-brick former Royal Herbert Hospital, which served the military from 1865 to 1978; it is now private apartments. The prominent red-brick former water tower further down is now

You could imagine yourself transported to the Alps as you approach the 'mountain hut' at the top of Oxleas Meadows.

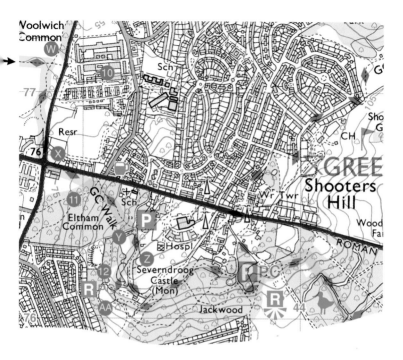

a spectacular private residence. Shooters Hill occupies part of the Roman Watling Street from Dover to London. The summit, at 432 feet (130 metres), is one of the highest points in Greater London.

Turn left by the 'new' red-brick, former police station of 1915 and keep on past the original yellow-brick one of 1852. At the start of Eltham Common **11**, bear slightly right across grass, towards a signpost in the trees about 30 yards in from the road. The Red Lion pub lies a short distance up Shooters Hill. Eltham Common is part of Shooters Hill Woods, a continuous belt of ancient woodland, together with Castlewood, Jackwood and Oxleas Wood, all traversed by the Capital Ring. They were acquired by the London County Council during the 1920s and 1930s, and have been designated a site of special scientific interest by the Nature Conservancy

Council because of the many rare species of flora and fauna found there.

Continue in the same direction into Castle Wood, climbing quite steeply on a gravel path with steps. At the top, by a car park **Y**, turn right along an access road, where you reach the highest point not only of Walk 1 but of the whole Capital Ring at altitude 419 feet (128 metres). At a fork **Z**, keep ahead to the intriguingly named Severndroog Castle **12**, which has recently been refurbished to include a tea room and toilets. The strange name of this triangular building comes from a fortress in India that was captured by Commodore Sir William James, who during the 18th century owned this land, then called Park Farm, later to become Eltham Park. After the commodore's death in 1784, his widow had the tower built as a memorial.

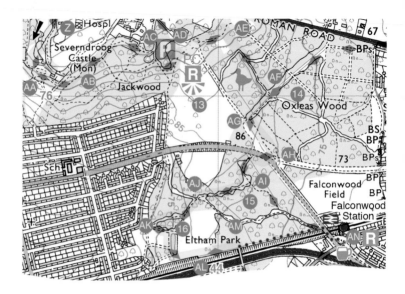

The rest of Walk 1 follows a rather complicated route, mostly in woodland, but well marked by GCW wooden posts. Beyond Severndroog, a path leads down to a flight of steps in several sections, with a total of about 70 steps. *These can be avoided on a GCW-signed alternative route, for which you should return to the fork **Z** just before Severndroog Castle, then turn sharp right down a tarmac track to pass a cottage. If you follow this alternative, skip the next paragraph to rejoin the main route by keeping ahead at the path junction **AB**.*

Continuing down the steps on the main route, with an extensive view across Sidcup into Kent, you reach a fork, where you can go either left or right. Go down more steps and keep ahead across a terrace, formerly the rose garden of Castlewood House, which stood here from the 1870s to the 1920s. On the far side go down yet more steps, then turn left at the foot along a level path on top of a disused reservoir **AA**. Pass through a

gap in an ivy-covered wall into Jackwood. Cross Stone Alley, an ancient track linking Shooters Hill with Eltham, then bear half-left up a slope, and turn left at the top by a large tree with a split trunk. At the next junction **AB**, turn right.

Go downhill to cross a small stream or ditch, then up again to join a tarmac path. At a fork, bear right along the lower of two paths through a grassed area, with a wall up to your left. This is the former ornamental garden of Jackwood House, which from the 1860s to the 1920s sat on what are now flowerbeds to your left. Bear left at the end of the gardens, then turn sharp right at the next junction **AC** to descend through more woodland and bear left to emerge into Oxleas Meadows **13**. Climb up to a pavilion **AD**, which sits atop the hill like an alpine mountain hut. It contains toilets and a café, from which you can admire the extensive view across south-east London to the North Downs.

Keep ahead past the pavilion and again at the tarmac path junction. Where the tarmac ends, keep ahead on the main rising track into Oxleas Wood **14**. At a massive tree with four great trunks **AE**, fork right downhill. In 25 yards, fork right again, deeper into the woods, ignoring side turnings, to reach a main signpost **AF** at a junction. Turn right along a broad, often muddy track, and in 150 yards, with the grass of Oxleas Meadows to your right, turn left **AG**. Follow a narrower track swinging left then right to reach Welling Way. Turn right to cross ahead at the lights over Rochester Way **AH**.

Go ahead on a narrow earth path into the trees of Eltham Park North **15**, here known as Shepherdleas Wood. In a few yards, turn right, parallel with the road, for 75 yards, then turn left, and in another 75 yards turn left again to another main signpost **AI**. Turn right here, then at a major crossing track **AJ** keep ahead on a path that bends left, with an open space to your left. Descend gently among trees to a junction, where you turn left into the open space. On reaching a tarmac path **AK**, turn left along it then shortly turn right beside the railings of Long Pond **16**, once a boating lake, now a quiet retreat for waterbirds, with good views towards the City of London, The Shard, Canary Wharf and Crystal Palace.

At the end of the pond, bear left, still on a tarmac path, to follow a high fence. The roar of traffic has been increasing steadily, and its source lies to your right in the shape of the A2 Rochester Way Relief Road, occasionally augmented by trains on the Dartford Loop line, out of sight in a

The three-sided Severndroog Castle was built in 1784 to commemorate the exploits of Commodore Sir William James.

cutting below. When the tarmac finishes **AL**, jink right then left along a wide, rolled-earth track in woodland, still beside the fence. In 200 yards you reach the wide, concrete Falconwood Footbridge **AM**, where Walk 1 of the Capital Ring ends. *To continue on Walk 2, turn right across the bridge into Eltham Park South.*

Capital Ring link to Falconwood Station and bus stops *(0.3 mile / 0.5 km). Do not cross the bridge but continue ahead beside the railway for 420 yards to Rochester Way. Turn right across the railway and cross at the refuge to Falconwood Station **AN** (toilets) and bus stops. The final 30 yards of this link provide the Capital Ring's only representation in the London Borough of Bexley.*

2 Falconwood to Grove Park

Distance 3.5 miles (5.6 km). Excludes Capital Ring links at each end: 0.3 miles (0.5 km) from Falconwood and 0.4 miles (0.7 km) to Grove Park..

Public transport The start of Walk 2 is 500 yards from Falconwood Station and bus stops. There is a link en route with Mottingham Station. The finish is 200 yards from bus stops and just under half a mile from Grove Park Station. All stations on this walk are in Travelcard Zone 4.

Surface and terrain This section undulates gently with some short, steep ascents but is mostly level. From Falconwood Station to the start on Falconwood Footbridge is mostly on a rolled-earth path. Falconwood Footbridge to Eltham: mostly paving or tarmac, with a short stretch on an earth path. Eltham to Middle Park: mostly dirt track. Middle Park to Grove Park: mostly paving or tarmac, but with 700 yards on an earth path and a stepped footbridge over a railway line.

Refreshments Falconwood, Eltham and Grove Park.

Toilets Eltham Park South, Eltham and Grove Park.

Refreshments and toilets are also available at Eltham Palace, but there is an admission charge (except for English Heritage members).

---

*Capital Ring link from Falconwood Station and bus stops (0.3 mile / 0.5 km). From Falconwood Station exit **A** (toilets) turn right along Lingfield Crescent and cross Rochester Way at the refuge. Ignore Green Chain Walk (GCW) signs to the left. Turn right to cross the railway, then turn left along a rolled-earth path beside the railway into woodland in Eltham Park North. In 420 yards you reach a wide concrete bridge **B**. You join the Capital Ring by turning left here.*

Walk 2 starts at Falconwood Footbridge **B** in the Royal Borough of Greenwich, and you are still sharing the route of the Green Chain Walk (GCW). The bridge leads over the railway line and A2 Rochester Way Relief Road into Eltham Park South **1**. This is an open and formal park, in complete contrast to the wooded and more natural Eltham Park North on Walk 1. Turn right at the main signpost, then immediately left to follow the tarmac path along the left-hand side of the park, with Eltham Warren Golf Course beyond the fence. *There are toilets and a refreshment kiosk in the red-brick building away to the right by some tennis courts.*

At the end of the park, cross then turn left along Glenesk Road **C**, near the site of the former mansion of Eltham Park. In 250 yards cross the busy A210 Bexley Road **D** at the zebra crossing. Continue ahead along a tarmac track called Butterfly Lane – take care, as it has no pavement ✱ and can be busy at times, being a cycle track, the approach to stables and a building site. At the end, by a gate **E**, bear right along an earth path to a triangular patch of grass with a main signpost. Bear right into Conduit Meadow and shortly you pass an odd little brick structure, which is Conduit Head **2**.

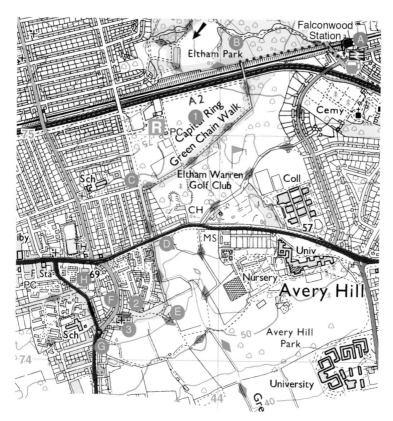

Surprisingly unprotected, it is in fact a Grade II listed building, which once housed sluices to control the flow of water from springs nearby to Eltham Palace. Continue ahead to Southend Crescent, with Holy Trinity Church **3** on your left. Consecrated in 1869, it contains the Gallipoli Chapel, a memorial to those who died in the World War I battle of that name. If you hear heavenly voices, it will probably be Eltham Choral Society, who perform regular concerts here.

Turn left along Southend Crescent **F** to a mini-roundabout **G** *(buses)*. Keep ahead to cross Footscray Road at a refuge (or traffic lights) then turn right up the left-

hand side of Footscray Road, passing St Thomas More Roman Catholic Comprehensive School. In 200 yards the Capital Ring goes left along North Park **H**, keeping to its left-hand pavement. In

Conduit Head used to house sluices that controlled the flow of water to Eltham Palace.

500 yards you pass Passey Place **I**, the nearest point to the facilities of Eltham High Street *(buses). There are toilets in Sainsbury's, through a car park on your right along Passey Place.* The town seems to breed great comedians: it has a theatre named after Bob Hope, who was born here in 1903 but emigrated with his family to the United States at the age of four, and Frankie Howerd spent much of his childhood here.

At the end of North Park, cross Court Road **J** at the refuge to the left, then continue in the same direction on the left-hand side of Tilt Yard Approach. At a grass area, where the original gatehouse to Eltham Palace was situated, cross over and turn left along Court Yard **K**, which used to be an outer courtyard of the palace. *A signed Green Chain Walk link with Eltham Station leads off to the right here.* Just before the present palace gate **L**, on your right, is a mustard-and-chocolate timber-framed building, dating from the early 16th century, which was the Lord Chancellor's Lodgings **4** – occasional residents included Cardinal Wolsey and Sir Thomas More. It has been converted into three houses: number 34 was the Parlour, 36 the Hall, and 38 the Great Chamber. Directly ahead now, across a moat, lies the Great Hall of Eltham Palace **5**, the principal country residence of the English monarchy for nearly 250 years, from the early 14th to the mid-16th centuries. It was surrounded by an extensive deer park and became a favourite resort for hunting. The Great Hall, with its impressive hammerbeam roof, was added during the 1470s. Henry VIII lost interest in Eltham, instead favouring Greenwich and Hampton Court, but Elizabeth I often stayed here. During the Civil War, the palace and gardens were ransacked and ruined by Cromwell's troops. In the 1930s, the palace was acquired by the Courtauld family, of textiles fame. They built a flamboyant new mansion for their own use, restored part of the moat, and created beautiful gardens. They moved out during World War II, and the hall was used as a military college until 1992. English Heritage have since restored the whole complex as a tourist attraction and function venue.

Eltham Palace

For nearly 250 years Eltham Palace was the principal country residence of the English monarchy. It can easily be visited from the Capital Ring.

From the gate of Eltham Palace, turn right down King John's Walk, a road with no pavement, so take care, especially at the bends. The route is thought to take its name from the French king Jean II, who exercised there while held captive during the 14th century, but gates along it are adorned with the white rose of the House of York, whose kings reigned 1461–85. Near the foot of the hill, beside a footpath junction **M**, turn left, still on the tarmac road with no pavement. Keep ahead past gates and stables on a gently rising track between fields – still King John's Walk. Now a grand view appears on your right of The Shard and other buildings in central London, also Canary Wharf and the yellow masts of the O_2 Arena. At the brow, in Middle Park now, you reach another main signpost. Continue down to and cross Middle Park Avenue *(buses)* to reach a grassed area **N**.

Capital Ring link with Mottingham Station (0.5 mile / 0.8 km). Turn left along Middle Park Avenue all the way to Court Road **O**, where you turn right to Mottingham Station **P**. If starting here, from the station's main exit go up the approach road, then at the main road turn left over the railway. In 70 yards turn left again along Middle Park Avenue **O**. Ignore GCW signs in this area. In 800 yards, halfway along a grass area (Joan Crescent) **N**, turn left along a concrete-lined path to join the Capital Ring.

Keep ahead along a concrete-lined path. This leads to a footbridge over a railway line, with 35 steps up and down. Cross the A20 Sidcup Road **Q** at the pedestrian crossing. Continue ahead along a tarmac path between houses and a field (still King John's Walk), crossing the boundary for a brief first visit to the London Borough of Bromley. In 200 yards you reach Mottingham Lane **R**. A little to your left here is Eltham College (see later) and its Gerald Moore Gallery, where occasional exhibitions are held. Cross to the main signpost then turn right up the far side for 450 yards. On your right at the top, opposite Eltham College Junior School, is Mottingham Farm **6**, now a riding school. Around the turn of the 20th century it was the home of Farmer Brown, a local character who adopted the typical

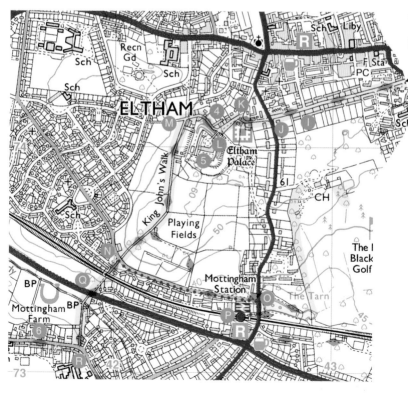

The moat at Eltham Palace, dating from the 14th century, was restored by the Courtauld family in the 1930s.

farmer's garb of smock and tall hat, and set a fine example by living to the age of 102 on a diet of whisky, ale, steak and cigars. At a right-hand bend, the route goes left along a footpath **S**, but note the large house ahead on your right, called Fairmount **7**. Now a residential home for the elderly, it was formerly the home of supreme cricketer W. G. Grace (1848–1915), as indicated on the blue plaque.

The narrow earth footpath runs straight at first, between paddocks on your right and, on your left, the playing fields of Eltham College, whose flag-topped tower **8** rises beyond. Former pupils of the college include Eric Liddell, the athlete of *Chariots of Fire* fame, and Mervyn Peake, author of the *Gormenghast* trilogy. This path can get very muddy after heavy rain, and is calf-deep in fallen leaves in late autumn and winter. It turns right then left between more paddocks and playing fields, known as College Meadow. You come to a railing, where the path bears left **T**. In a concrete channel below is the infant Quaggy River **9**, a tributary of

the Ravensbourne. At College Meadow Pavilion (part of the Eltham College complex), bear right along its access road, which crosses into the London Borough of Lewisham, to a main signpost on Marvels Lane **U**, the end of Walk 2. *To continue on to Walk 3, turn right along Marvels Lane.*

Capital Ring link to Grove Park Station *(0.4 mile / 0.7 km). Carefully cross Marvels Lane and keep ahead along a footpath left of the Quaggy River. At Chinbrook Road go over the zebra crossing **V** then turn right uphill. At the top (automatic toilets) turn left to Grove Park Station **W**, with bus stops nearby.*

3 Grove Park to Crystal Palace

Distance 7.7 miles (12.4 km). Excludes Capital Ring link of 0.4 miles (0.7 km) from Grove Park Station to the start.

Public transport Walk 3 starts in Marvels Lane, just under half a mile from Grove Park Station and bus station. Buses serve Marvels Lane and Chinbrook Road, 200 yards from the start. The route passes New Beckenham and Penge East Stations, and there are links with Ravensbourne, Beckenham Junction, Kent House and Penge West Stations. The walk ends at Crystal Palace Station, close to bus stops. All stations on this walk are in Travelcard Zone 4 except Crystal Palace which is in Zones 3 and 4.

Surface and terrain Grove Park to Downham: mostly level paving or tarmac, with one stepped footbridge. Downham to New Beckenham: mostly on tarmac or rolled-earth paths or tracks through Beckenham Place Park with short ascents and descents, sometimes steep. New Beckenham to Penge: level tarmac or paving with one stepped footbridge. Penge to Crystal Palace Park: tarmac or paving with some short steep ascents and descents. The route climbs steadily inside Crystal Palace Park.

Refreshments Grove Park, Downham, Beckenham Place Park, Penge, Crystal Palace Park, Anerley Hill.

Toilets Grove Park, Downham, Beckenham Place Park, Crystal Palace Park.

*Capital Ring link from Grove Park Station (0.4 miles / 0.7 km). From the station exit **A** turn right along Baring Road. At the traffic lights (automatic toilets) turn right down Chinbrook Road. At the foot of the hill, go left over the zebra crossing and keep ahead along a footpath on thre right of the Quaggy River. In 200 yards at Marvels Lane **B**, turn left along the left-hand pavement, with Walk 2 of the Capital Ring coming in along the drive opposite. Cross over at the refuge, then continue in the same direction on the far side. You join the Capital Ring here.*

*To avoid the stepped footbridge at point **2**, from Grove Park Station go ahead along Downham Way, then take the first right, Reigate Road, for 700 yards to meet the footpath off the bridge at the third left-hand bend **E**.*

Walk 3 of the Capital Ring starts in Marvels Lane **B** in the London Borough of Lewisham, still keeping company with the Green Chain Walk (GCW). Pass the former Grove Park Hospital, now redeveloped as a residential area. After a group of trees marking one end of Sydenham Cottages Nature Reserve, turn right past Grove Park Library. Cross Somertrees Avenue **C** at the refuge, turn right then cross and turn left along the right-hand side of Coopers Lane, at first on grass. In 250 yards you reach the A2212 Baring Road **D**. Turn right and cross at the second refuge. Turn right then immediately left along a tarmac footpath and cycleway called Railway Children Walk **1** after the famous book by E. Nesbitt (Mrs Edith Bland), who lived nearby. Shortly, you pass Grove Park Nature Reserve **2**. Among the unusual species that can be spotted here are green ring-necked parakeets, though these are becoming a fairly common sight in London's open spaces.

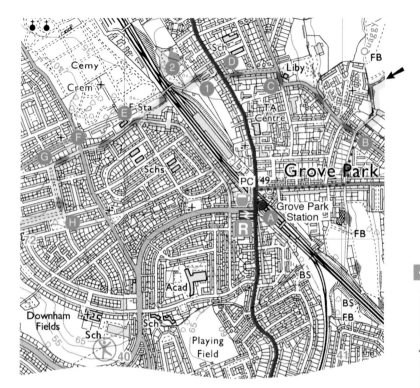

Cross the footbridge (25 steps up, 36 down) over the main railway line from London to the Kent coast. A major rail disaster occurred to the right of the bridge in 1967, when a derailment resulted in 49 fatalities. Continue along the footpath through a landscaped area, with Hither Green Cemetery to your right. At Reigate Road **E** keep ahead along the right-hand pavement, passing a children's playground and Downham Fire Station with its training tower. At the main road, Northover **F**, cross with care via the central reservation. Keep ahead along Whitefoot Terrace, then in 150 yards turn left up Woodbank Road **G**. This has two roadways on either side of a grassy, wooded central strip, and you can walk either on the grass or along the right-hand pavement. Pass Bideford and Ilfracombe Roads, then turn right along Undershaw Road **H**, with a similar strip separating it from Shaw

Ring-necked parakeets are now a common sight in London's parks and open spaces, including Grove Park Nature Reserve.

Road. At the end, cross Moorside Road **I** and go left then right along a tarmac footpath which is the Downham Woodland Walk **3**, where dogs should be kept on a lead. This footpath runs for over a mile along a narrow strip of woodland, a remnant of the Great North Wood. Until London began to expand, this vast forest stretched some 7 miles (11 km) along the hills between what are now Croydon and Deptford, and you will encounter other remnants further along the Capital Ring.

The Woodland Walk crosses several roads. At the first, Downderry Road **J**, continue to the left of a postbox and railings beside some cottages to re-enter the wood. At this point, you cross the Greenwich Meridian Line and then closely follow it for 400 yards – it will be encountered again on Walk 14. The path now winds between houses and crosses Oakshade Road **K** and Haddington Road **L**. At the end of the path, by a wooden train, cross Oakridge Road to the A21 Bromley Road **M** at Downham.

Go over the zebra crossing, then turn half-left along Old Bromley Road, crossing to the right-hand pavement. *At Downham Way **N**, there is an automatic toilet at the main road to your left.* Cross

Brangbourne Road, then after 50 yards turn right through the entrance **O** into Beckenham Place Park **4**, once the private estate of Beckenham Place (see below). This large park and nature reserve is open grassland here, but becomes well wooded later. Follow the tarmac footpath along the right-hand edge, shortly crossing a humped footbridge. Below it is the River Ravensbourne **5**, flowing from Keston Ponds, near Bromley, through Catford and Lewisham to the Thames at Deptford Creek. Its name is supposed to derive from Roman times, when Caesar's army camped near Keston: soldiers searching for water saw ravens frequenting a certain spot and discovered a spring there.

In 250 yards the Capital Ring turns sharp left at a path junction **P** in a copse. *At this point, you can continue ahead for 300 yards to Beckenham Hill Station **Q**, though this is not a formal Capital Ring link.* The path bends right up a ramp to cross a railway line (beware traffic using a waste-disposal site nearby). The tarmac peters out as you bear left beside Beckenham Place Park Golf Course to continue on a gravel path into ancient woodland. In 200 yards fork right, ignoring turnings into the golf course. In another 150 yards fork left, then, at a T-junction **R**, turn right and climb up a track for 150 yards to a path intersection **S**. A GCW alternative route avoiding imminent steps continues ahead, but the Capital Ring main route runs right, leading in 125 fairly steep yards with some widely spaced steps to a main signpost **T** and information board at the centre of Beckenham Place Park, where you bear right.

This wooden train leads you out of the Downham Woodland Walk

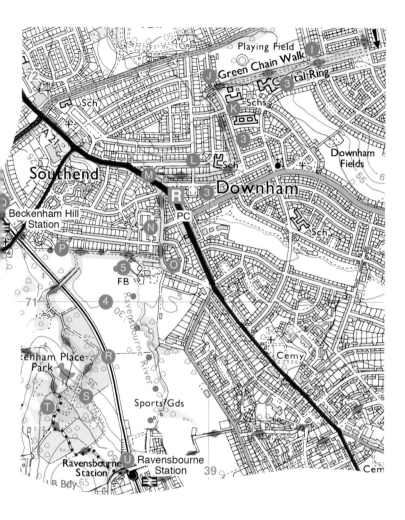

Capital Ring link with Ravensbourne Station (0.4 miles / 0.7 km). This follows a branch of the GCW. Turn left at the main signpost **T**, and shortly keep ahead past another one. In 80 yards fork left, then in 60 yards turn right. At an open space turn left along a tarmac path, and back in the trees turn right down a gravel track. At the road turn left to Ravensbourne Station **U**. If starting here, from the station exit turn left up Crab Hill, then in 60 yards turn right into Beckenham Place Park. Follow the sunken track ahead. At a T-junction turn left to a tarmac path into an open space. Shortly, turn right into the wood, then turn left at the next junction. In 60 yards turn right and keep ahead to a main signpost. The track bears left to another main signpost **T** at the centre of the park, where you join the Capital Ring by turning left.

John Cator's 18th-century mansion in Beckenham Place Park.

Follow a track which passes a golf green and tee, swings left and descends to cross a little stream. It then climbs towards the mansion, passing a white-painted giant squirrel sculpture. The old stable block on your right suffered a bad fire recently but there are plans to rebuild it to provide a visitor centre, café and toilets. The flower beds here are worth a very short diversion.

You come to a path junction **V**, immediately before the mansion, Beckenham Place **6**, *which has a licensed café and toilets*. The park and an earlier building were acquired in 1773 by John Cator, a wealthy timber merchant. He rebuilt the mansion, incorporating bits of his previous home,

Wricklemarsh Park, near Blackheath, including the splendid portico. The house and park were acquired for public use in 1927 by London County Council. They developed the public golf course, with its clubhouse in the mansion, now a Grade II listed building. Unfortunately, the mansion is rather run down but there is a visitor centre which opens on Sunday afternoons.

Turn right along a path between bushes to a driveway, then turn left beside a car park. With the grand portico of the mansion on your left, turn right along a tarmac path. This swings right then left to lead out of the park on to a road **W** – Beckenham Hill to your right, Southend Road to your left. Now back in the London Borough of Bromley, turn left along A2105 Southend Road for 200 yards. Cross over at the refuge just before Calverley Close and continue along the far pavement to the junction with Stumps Hill Lane **X**, where you turn right.

Where Stumps Hill Lane becomes unmade, keep ahead down a stretch with no pavement. The Capital Ring now threads a route between the fringes of Beckenham to your left and Sydenham to your right. Ahead lies one of Kent County Cricket Club's grounds, and you have a fine view beyond it towards Crystal Palace, where this walk ends. At the foot, cross then turn left along Worsley Bridge Road **Y** past the main sign. Away to the right, in front of another imposing pavilion, is the

training ground of Crystal Palace Football Club. At the T-junction **Z** cross Brackley Road and turn right.

*Capital Ring link with Beckenham Junction Station and Croydon Tramlink (0.6 miles / 0.9 km). Turn left up Brackley Road, then turn right at the top along Southend Road. In 600 yards, keep ahead past Waitrose to the next traffic lights, turn right along Rectory Road then immediately right again along the approach to Beckenham Junction Station (toilets) **AA** and tram stop. If starting here, from the main station exit bear left to the traffic lights then turn sharp left along the High Street. Pass Waitrose, then continue ahead along Southend Road. In 600 yards turn left down Brackley Road. You join the Capital Ring by keeping ahead at the junction with Worsley Bridge Road **Z**.*

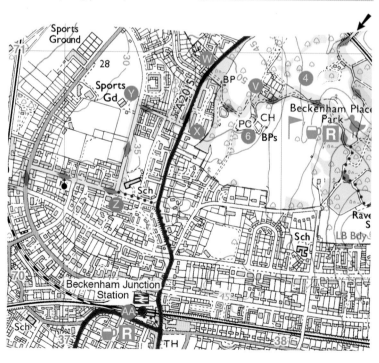

You are now heading for the stately spire of St Paul's Church **7**, New Beckenham. At the end of Brackley Road, cross Copers Cope Road **AB**, named after a large farm that once occupied this area. Turn left, then shortly turn right along Park Road to pass through a ramped subway **AC** under New Beckenham Station. The original station lay to the left; it was replaced by the current one, to the right, in 1904.

You emerge from the subway for the first of three brief encounters with the long and straight Lennard Road. With the HSBC Sports & Social Club on your right, in 50 yards turn left into King's Hall Road **AD**, using the right-hand pavement. In 275 yards, opposite Bridge Road **AE**, turn right between house numbers 173 and 175 along a tarmac path into Cator Park **8**, formerly the private Kent House Pleasure Gardens.

You cross two streams – The Beck, then Chaffinch Brook – which merge a little way to your right, inside the park, to form the Pool River, a tributary of the Ravensbourne. At the main signpost **AF** at the centre of the park, you come to a shared-use track for cyclists and pedestrians, where you turn right. This is part of the Waterlink Way, developed by Sustrans, from the Thames at Deptford Creek through South London into Surrey. *The link with Kent House Station begins here – see next page.*

Continue along the shared-use track (keep left) to the point where it turns right, then keep ahead to the corner of the park and back onto Lennard Road **AH**, dominated here by Harris Girls' Academy, formerly Cator Park School. Turn left and go over the zebra crossing, then turn left to the traffic lights **AI**. Cross over then turn right

In Cator Park the Ca Ring briefly joins the Waterlink Way cycle

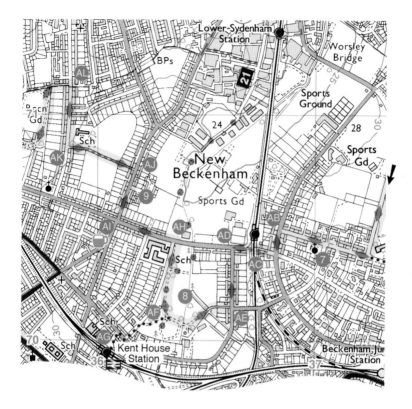

along Kent House Road *(the Kent House Tavern lies 130 yards to your left)*. About 100 yards along on your right, Beckett Walk covers the site of

Capital Ring link with Kent House Station *(0.2 miles/ 0.4 km)*. At the signpost, bear half-left out of Cator Park. Cross and turn left along Aldersmead Road, then turn right to cross Kings Hall Road at the refuge. Turn left along the unmade Kent House Station Approach and go through the subway **AG** to the station platforms. If starting here, from the platforms follow signs to Kings Hall Road, where you turn right, then left along Aldersmead Road to enter Cator Park. At the central signpost **AF**, turn left past the wooden pavilion onto the Capital Ring.

Kent House **9**, which gave its name to the area and the station. The name resulted from it being at one time the first building in Kent on the road out of London. It dated from the 13th century and through most of its existence was a farmhouse. In the early 20th century, it became a nursing home, which was demolished in 1957.

In a further 100 yards, between house numbers 148 and 150, turn left along a narrow, fenced footpath **AJ** leading between school playing fields to Cator Road **AK**. The spire to your left is Holy Trinity Church. Cross over, then turn right for 275 yards, passing Woodbastwick Road. Just past number 57 (The Woodfields) **AL**, this becomes

*Iguanodon in the Dinosaur
Area of Crystal Palace Park.*

Trewsbury Road as it crosses into the London Borough of Lewisham; however, you just about stay in Bromley by turning left along an unmade driveway. At the end, turn left along a tarmac path along the left-hand side of Alexandra Recreation Ground **10**, opened to the public in 1891 and named after Queen Alexandra, wife of King Edward VII. At a pavilion, turn right between a bowling green and a disused drinking fountain. Pass a house inside the park, then turn left into Maitland Road **AM**, keeping ahead along its left-hand side.

At the end, for the third time, is Lennard Road **AN**, now much busier as part of the A213. *To avoid a stepped footbridge later, from Maitland Road keep ahead along Parish Lane, then in 250 yards turn right along Penge Lane. Take the first right, Queen Adelaide Road, then right at St John's Road to Penge East Station **AO**. Bear left past the footbridge along Station Road.*

Otherwise, turn right along Lennard Road to the next junction (Newlands Park) and cross at the refuge. Turn left to cross Venner Road at a second refuge, then keep ahead past some shops to cross the footbridge (25 steps) at Penge East Station **AO** (toilets). Looking left as you cross the footbridge, the building that protrudes into the far platform used to be the cottage of the keeper of the level crossing which once linked the roads on either side. On the far side, take the right-hand steps down to the station forecourt. Cross over then turn right along Station Road, passing a building (a former pub), with its vast mural, and the dainty little Good Shepherd Church **11**, established in 1887 as the Holy Trinity mission house (with no incumbent of its own). In 100 yards turn left along Kingswood Road **AP**, following the right-hand pavement to A234 Penge High Street **AQ**, where you cross at the lights. The name Penge is unusual for this area, having a Celtic origin – Penceat or Pencoed, meaning wood end.

Cross, then turn right up Penge High Street to pass under two railway bridges **AR** sandwiching the Bridge House pub which contains a small theatre. The first

Capital Ring link with Penge West Station (0.1 miles / 0.1 km). Between the bridges **AR**, turn left along Anerley Park to find Penge West Station **AS** on your left (toilets). If starting here, from the station exit go ahead to the road (Anerley Park) then turn right. At Penge High Street turn left under the second bridge **AR**.

bridge carries the main line from London Bridge to the Sussex coast. This section was one of the earliest railway lines in London, built in 1839 for the London and Croydon Railway. It was originally operated by atmospheric traction, by which trains were vacuum-drawn through a continuous pipe. The second bridge was built in 1854 for the branch to Crystal Palace.

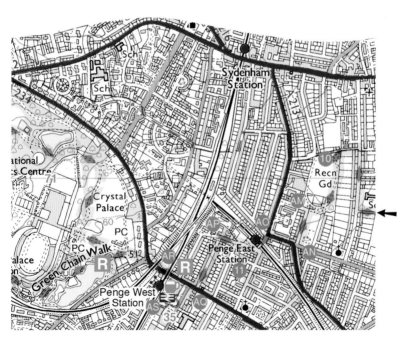

Cross Thicket Road and go through the Penge entrance **AT** into Crystal Palace Park **12**. Keep ahead past a car park to a main signpost **AU**, with an information centre and toilets to your right and a café to your left (the café is due to be rebuilt in the near future). Crystal Palace Park was created in 1854 to provide a new site for the great glass exhibition hall that had previously stood in Hyde Park for the Great Exhibition of 1851. The Crystal Palace offered a fantastic array of displays, circuses, concerts and shows, but although it was one of the most popular tourist attractions of its day, it never recovered its costs. In 1911, the Crystal Palace Company was declared bankrupt, and two years later the palace became the property of the nation. Then, in 1936, the building was destroyed by a spectacular fire; the site and terraces at the top of the park have since lain desolate. Crystal Palace Park is managed by the London Borough of Bromley, who are currently engaged in refurbishment of the Grade I listed dinosaurs. More infomation can be found on the website: www.crystalpalacepark.org.uk.

The Capital Ring's route in Crystal Palace Park has returned to its original direct line through the Dinosaur Area, though at times you may have to follow a more circuitous alternative to the north. This is because the Dinosaur Area opens later and closes earlier (about half an hour in each case) than the rest of the park; opening times can be checked on website http://bit.ly/Hx7qpp. *If this affects you, from the main sign and information centre keep ahead up the central avenue, then follow the Capital Ring signs, which follow the park perimeter, close to the site of the original Crystal Palace 15, to Crystal Palace Station AX.*

From the main sign by the park information centre **AU** bear half-left up a path to the park café. Go through a gate and turn left past the café, through a second gate. The 'Gorilla' sculpture on your left was created in 1961 by David Wynne. Bear right at a fence and follow it round to the left into the Dinosaur Area **13**, where sculptures are scattered around the lakes – information boards describe them in detail. The word 'dinosaur', coined in 1842 by the palæontologist Richard Owen, is of Greek origin and means 'terrible lizard', though not all the sculptures are dinosaurs in this sense. Indeed, beside a lake, you come face-to-face with a megaloceros, also referred to as the Irish elk, as the best preserved remains of the species were found in peat bogs in Ireland, where it lived until about 10,000 years ago. Pedal-boats can be hired on the lake.

Benjamin Waterhouse-Hawkins created the sculptures in 1852, guided by Richard Owen, based on the latest archaeological evidence, though later research has proved them to be wildly inaccurate. They have been recently refurbished. Keep

Crystal Palace Park

A quarter of the way round the Capital Ring lies Crystal Palace Park. Celebrate with a cup of tea in the park café, then admire its charmingly misinterpreted dinosaur sculptures basking along the lake shores.

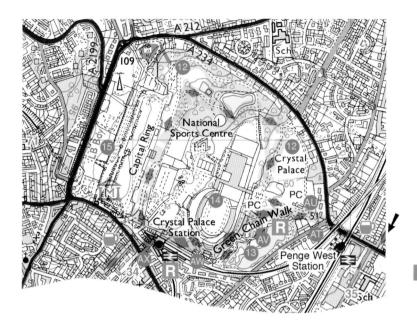

ahead past the beast with huge antlers. At the next junction, with information board **AV**, turn right to cross a bridge, then left to skirt a small hill. Turn left again beside information boards, one describing a representation of geological strata, passed as you cross a long footbridge. Keep ahead on the far side to encounter the main group of monsters lurking on islands in the lake over to your left.

Turn right at the next junction, rising steadily and passing the Crystal Palace Park Centre of Capel Manor College **AW**. Capel Manor, one of the country's leading establishments for outdoor studies, has its main base near Enfield and has set up a number of satellites for specialist subjects; this one provides courses on animal care.

Turn left out of the Dinosaur Area through a gate. Keep ahead up a steep rise. To your right now are the great stands and soaring floodlights of the Crystal Palace Athletics Stadium **14**, part of the National Sports Centre. And of course the Crystal Palace transmitter, beaming most of the main television and radio channels; at nearly 720 feet (219 metres) it is one of London's tallest structures, though with its summit at 1,097 feet (335 metres) above sea level it could claim to be a mountain! Follow the path round to a broad gravel area and turn left to Crystal Palace Station **AX** and the end of Walk 3. A recent extension of the Green Chain Walk continues ahead here, to Nunhead, and at last the Capital Ring strikes out on its own. You pass the imposing station building, built in 1854 to cope with crowds heading for the grand exhibition hall. It was closed in the 1980s but was restored and reopened in 2012, with a café *(toilets on Platform 1).*

4 Crystal Palace to Streatham

Distance 4.1 miles (6.6 km). Excludes Capital Ring link of 0.1 miles (0.2 km) to Streatham Common Station.

Public transport Walk 4 starts at the exit from Crystal Palace Station with bus stops nearby. It has a link with Streatham Station, and finishes 200 yards from Streatham Common Station and bus stops. There are buses at Beulah Hill. Crystal Palace Station is in Travelcard Zones 3 and 4. Streatham and Streatham Common are in Zone 3.

Surface and terrain On tarmac or paving throughout. However, walkers with dogs will have to make a diversion of 200 yards on grass at Norwood Grove. Crystal Palace to Church Road: includes a long and very steep ascent. Church Road to Beulah Hill: includes a very steep descent and a fairly steep ascent. Beulah Hill to Streatham: mostly level but with two fairly steep descents and one fairly steep ascent.

Refreshments Anerley Hill, Church Road, The Rookery, Streatham.

Toilets Westow Road, The Rookery, Streatham Common.

Walk 4 starts at Crystal Palace Station **A** in the London Borough of Bromley. From the station exit turn left down Crystal Palace Station Road to Anerley Hill **B**. Cross at the lights then turn right past Retro Joe Café (the former Paxton Arms Hotel). Turn left into Pleydell Avenue. You are now in one of the hilliest parts of South London and will soon climb steeply over two ridges.

At the end of Pleydell Avenue, bear right then left through Palace Square **C**. Keep ahead up a steep, zigzag footpath beside a playground and grass area. Ahead is Belvedere Road **D**, apparently so named after the houses it contained – *belvedere* means 'beautiful view' in Italian. Look left and you will see two such houses, with their rooftop belvederes, built in the late 19th century. Cross Belvedere Road and turn right past the handsome Belvedere Court.

Number 22 on the left has a plaque to Benjamin Waterhouse Hawkins, a 19th-century sculptor. Shortly turn left into Tudor Road **E**, where there are more fine old residences, especially Tudor House and Barton House. Another tall mast rises ahead – this one is the South Norwood transmitter, a back-up for Crystal Palace. At the end, pass Lansdowne Place then turn right into Fox Hill **F**. At A212 Church Road **G** turn right, go over the zebra crossing, then turn right to enter Westow Park **1**, where you pass into the London Borough of Croydon. You are now in the district of Norwood, which takes its name from the ancient Great North Wood (see Walk 3). *A short distance ahead now is Crystal Palace Triangle, with its many pubs, cafés and bus station.*

Descend the steep hill through Westow Park to a gate, where you turn left, but look up to your right to see the spire of the Greek Orthodox Church of Saints Constantine and Helen **2**. *For toilets, go through the gate, turn left and up the staircase (42 steps) between the garden centre and Sainsbury's car park.* Continuing through the park, to your right beyond the trees is a long red-brick building, which was formerly part of the Royal Normal College for blind children and is now a training and family-support centre for Barnardo's **3**. Bear right at a fork, then left to pass a playground, and go round two sides of a grass square to reach a road (College Green). Turn right then shortly cross and turn left along Harold Road **H**, which is the centre of a conservation area containing substantial and decorative Victorian houses.

Cross and turn right along Chevening Road *(buses)* beside Upper Norwood Recreation Ground **4**. In 100 yards turn left into the park, then turn right at the junction along a path, which runs parallel to the road, where you pass a disused granite drinking fountain, dated 1891. Rejoin the road, passing Rockmount Primary School, then turn left into the park once more **I**. A boulder on your right is one of 20 placed aound the London Borough of Croydon to mark its 80th anniversary in 2015. Go all the way across, passing a pavilion, while up to your left is the South Norwood transmitter.

On the far side of the park, turn right along Eversley Road **J**, still beside the open space. Away to your right, two little spires mark the Church and Convent of the Faithful Virgin on Central Hill **5**.

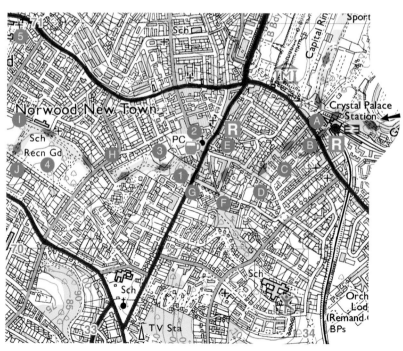

Biggin Wood is one of the largest remnants of ancient Great North Wood, which once extended for 7 miles between Croydon and Dartford.

At the end, turn left up Hermitage Road **K** to the top and A215 Beulah Hill **L** *(buses)*. Go over the zebra crossing, then turn right. The little house with the green tiled roof was the lodge of a mansion called Woodlands.

Along Beulah Hill, number 75 has a black plaque to indicate that from 1946 to 1973 it was the home of Joan and Alan Warwick, founders of the Norwood Society. There are many more fine residences along the left-hand side. Cross Downsview Road **M**, look right for a view of The Shard and the City of London, and in 300 yards turn left down Biggin Hill **N**, using the left-hand pavement. A short way down on your left is a modern residential development called Dickens Wood Close. The name is significant, as it occupies the site of Springfield **6**, where Charles Dickens stayed and set the scene for David

Copperfield to meet Dora Spenlow. And opposite, continuing the theme, is Havisham Place. Now a broad vista opens up across the tall buildings of Croydon's town centre to the North Downs. After passing some allotments, cross via a refuge to the opposite pavement, then in 50 yards, opposite number 47, turn right along a footpath **O**. This leads past tennis courts into Biggin Wood **7**, another remnant of the Great North Wood.

Continue ahead along a tarmac footpath to the far side of the wood. At the road, proceed to a junction **P** then bear right along Covington Way, using the right-hand pavement. Stenton Covington (1856–1935) was a very active local campaigner who did a great deal for this area. Keep ahead at two crossroads, with Norbury Hill and Christian Fields. At Gibson's Hill **Q** turn right through a gate into a park called

Norwood Grove **8**. Follow a narrow tarmac path that winds up through the park. At a fork keep ahead to reach a main sign **R**. *Dogs are not permitted inside the enclosure; they must be taken along a signed Capital Ring diversion on grass to the right, outside the fence.*

Dogless walkers may pass through the gate ahead, then immediately turn left. You soon have a fine view to your right of the mansion **9**, also called Norwood Grove, and its gardens. To your left, the huge, white building in the distance is St Helier Hospital. Keep ahead beside the fence and pass through an arched rose arbour. At the terrace, *toilets ahead*, turn right to go around two sides of the mansion and its orangery. Norwood Grove, the park, was once part of Streatham Common. Norwood Grove, the mansion, known locally as

the White House, was originally much larger – only the east wing of the original building survives. It was built during the 1840s for Arthur Anderson, joint founder of P&O (Peninsular and Oriental Steam Navigation Company), MP for the Shetland Isles, and said to have been a keen early supporter of Crystal Palace Football Club. A plaque at the corner pays tribute to former residents and local benefactors Mr and Mrs Frederick Nettlefold

At the far corner of the mansion, go through a gate **S**, where the dog diversion rejoins the route. Turn left through another gate, then immediately left into a drive. Bear right past a barrier and continue along the fenced Copgate Path to a lodge. Here you cross into the London Borough of Lambeth: the boundary is marked by a tiny stream that feeds the River Graveney,

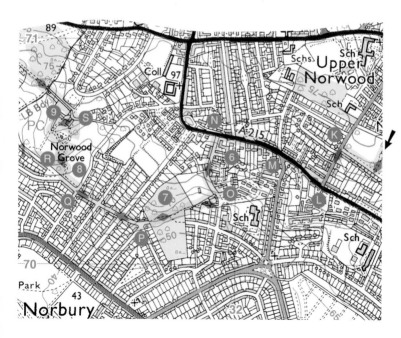

itself a tributary of the Wandle, and a line of 400-year-old oak trees **10**. Continue along the drive, now on Streatham Common **11**, to reach a car park, with The Rookery gardens **12** on your left, featured in many guides to the best public gardens. South-west London is blessed with a string of extensive commons, most of which were saved from development by a variety of bodies during the 19th century. This did not, however, save them from being sliced up by roads and railways, and most now lie in several separate pieces. All these commons were once wild areas, owned by the local squire, where people from the surrounding villages had certain rights, including grazing animals and collecting firewood, berries and nuts. Four are crossed by the Capital Ring, Streatham Common being the first.

At the road (Streatham Common South) **T**, bear left to pass the San Remo café, *beside which is an automatic toilet.* Cross the road to the next part of the common, noting the old granite water trough, one of many installed around London by the Metropolitan Drinking Fountain and Cattle Trough Association. It is now a planter. The seat nearby has a Millennium topograph set into its concrete base. Bear left down the common on a narrow tarmac footpath towards A23 Streatham High Road. The church tower ahead belongs to Streatham's Parish Church of Immanuel and St Andrew **13**. *Nearby are The Bull pub and a Sainsbury's with café and toilets.* Shortly before reaching the main road, bear half-right on a tarmac path **U**, then right again to walk parallel to the road.

Norwood Grove and its lovely gardens near Streatham Common.

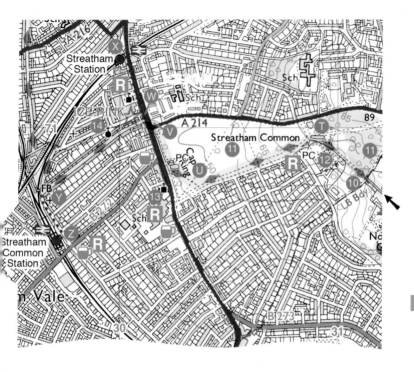

There are toilets beside the playground on your right. To your left, across the High Road, stands The Greyhound, dating from the early 18th century – a former coaching inn that served stagecoaches on the London to Brighton run. At a road called Streatham Common North, cross ahead to Streatham Memorial Garden **V**, then cross left over Streatham High Road *(buses)* to the junction with Lewin Road **W**. Streatham High Road is one of the longest shopping centres in London, stretching for 1¹/₂ miles. *Nearby are the Streatham Ice and Leisure Centre, home to the Streatham Redskins Ice Hockey team and a vast Tesco Extra – both have a café and toilets.*

*Capital Ring link to Streatham Station (0.2 miles / 0.3 km). Turn right along Streatham High Road to Streatham Station **X** (ladies and disabled toilets). If starting here, from the station exit turn right along Streatham High Road for 300 yards to the junction with Lewin Road **W**, cross it and turn right along the left-hand pavement.*

Keep ahead along the left-hand side of Lewin Road. You pass the red-brick Streatham Baptist Church **14**. Walk 4 ends at the junction with Estreham Road **Y**, where you can turn left for 200 yards to Streatham Common Station **Z** *(toilets)* or a little further for buses in Greyhound Lane. *To continue on Walk 5 turn right along Estreham Road.*

5 Streatham to Wimbledon Park

Distance 5.5 miles (8.8 km). Excludes a Capital Ring link of 0.1 miles (0.2 km) from Streatham Common Station.

Public transport The start of Walk 5 is 200 yards from Streatham Common Station and bus stops. The route passes Earlsfield and Wandsworth Common Stations, and there is a link with Balham Station. The finish is at Wimbledon Park Station and 250 yards from bus stops. All statiions on this walk are in Travelcard Zone 3.

Surface and terrain Almost all of this walk is on level paving or tarmac, with a very short stretch of grit path. There is a gentle ascent at the end.

Refreshments Tooting Bec Common, Balham, Wandsworth Common, Trinity Road, Earlsfield and Wimbledon Park.

Toilets Streatham Common Station, Tooting Bec Common, Balham and Wandsworth Common.

Capital Ring link from Streatham Common Station (0.1 miles / 0.2 km). From the main station exit A turn left through the car park and continue ahead along Estreham Road to the junction with Lewin Road. Here you join the Capital Ring, which comes along Lewin Road, by keeping ahead along Estreham Road.

Walk 5 starts at the junction of Lewin Road and Estreham Road **B** in the London Borough of Lambeth then continues along Estreham Road. To your left is a busy intersection of railway lines known as Streatham Junction **1**. It is used mostly by commuter trains, but the lower line with the faster trains is the Brighton Line, made famous by the classic short film of 1952 called 'London to Brighton in Four Minutes', filmed in fast motion from the driver's cab. The

line was opened in 1846 for the London, Brighton and South Coast Railway, and now also carries the brightly coloured Gatwick Express trains. In 220 yards turn left through a subway (mind your head) under the railway into Potters Lane **C**, where some pleasant dwellings appear to tolerate the railway mayhem, then turn right along Conyers Road.

Shortly on your left now lies an oddity: a yellow-brick Moorish temple, topped with several green copper cupolas, which is in fact Thames Water's Streatham Pumping Station **2**, built in 1888 for the Southwark & Vauxhall Waterworks Company. It is the first of several eccentric pumping stations that you will encounter along the route. Further on, at number 14, look out for the rather startling stained-glass window depicting a woman watching a departing sailing ship. At the end of Conyers Road cross A216 Mitcham Lane **D** – use the zebra crossing to the right – and keep ahead along tree-lined Riggindale Road. On your right is Streatham Methodist Church, built in 1900, which has a very wide, barrel-vaulted ceiling. At the end of the road, bear left on a footpath up a bank leading to A214 Tooting Bec Road **E**, with Tooting Common Woodlands opposite.

Turn left over the railway, entering as you do so the London Borough of Wandsworth, and cross Aldrington Road **F** then use the traffic lights to cross the main road. Turn left on the far side, past the approach to Tooting Bec Lido **3**. Opened in 1906, it is one of the largest swimming pools in Europe at 100 yards long and 33 yards wide. In 1936, following the fashion of the day, it was rebuilt in 'lido' style, taking this name from a fashionable bathing beach near Venice, with a large open-air pool and a paddling pool surrounded by extensive sunbathing areas.

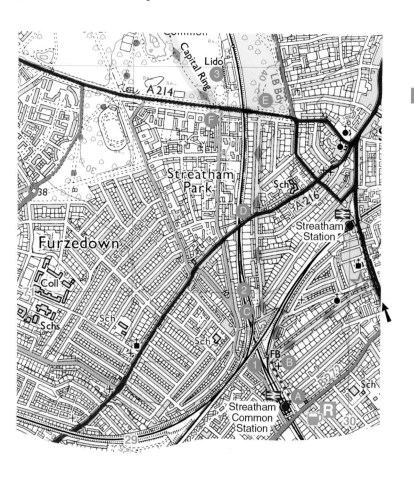

Immediately bear half-right along a tarmac footpath onto the southern part of Tooting Bec Common **4**. The name Bec comes from the granting of this parish to the abbey of St Mary de Bec in Normandy during the 12th century. There are actually two Tooting Commons, Graveney and Bec; the Capital Ring crosses the latter. Halfway across, behind a copse, lies a lake with a viewing platform. The park café *(toilet)* lies off to the left a little further on. At the road, Bedford Hill **G**, named after the Duke of Bedford who used to own much of this area, cross at the lights and continue ahead across the

northern part of the common (shared cycle track, keep left). Soon you bear left, between houses to your left and the Brighton Line again to your right. In 80 yards turn left by a notice board **H** along a short, fenced footpath.

Cross Culverden Road and go ahead along Fontenoy Road. Back at Bedford Hill **I**, turn right to cross at the refuge, then turn right and immediately left into Ritherdon Road, following the left-hand pavement. Pass Carminia and Childebert Roads, then cross over and turn right along Cloudesdale Road **J**, using the right-hand pavement. At the end, cross and turn left along Elmfield

Playing gol⌇
Tooting Bec Comm⌇
in the 19⌇

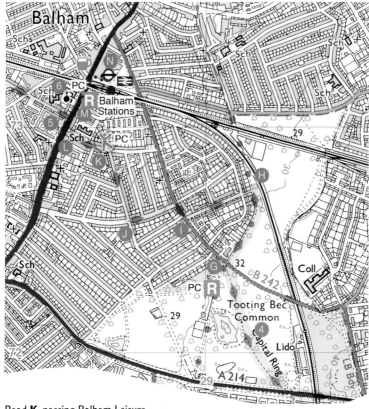

Road **K**, passing Balham Leisure Centre, *which has toilets.* Pass Ravenstone Primary School to reach Balham High Road **L** *(buses),* opposite Du Cane Court **5**. Despite its rather bland exterior, Du Cane Court is one of the most elegant apartment blocks in South London, dating from the Art Deco period of the 1930s. Turn right to the traffic lights **M**. *There are several cafés along here and the J. D. Wetherspoon pub The Moon Under Water is next to Balham Station.*

Cross Balham High Road at the traffic lights. Nearby is Balham's parish church of St Mary and St John the Divine **6**, dating from 1808. Projecting in front is

> ***Capital Ring link with Balham Station*** *(0.1 miles / 0.2 km). Keep ahead past the traffic lights to the railway bridge. Balham National Rail (toilets) and London Underground stations **N** are on the right past the bridge. If starting here, from the station exits go under the railway bridge for 200 yards to the traffic lights **M**.*

an unusual domed baptistry, and the original bell still chimes the hours and announces services. Turn left and immediately right along Balham Park Road, then in 200 yards cross

One of the ponds on Wandsworth Common has a boardwalk, which provides an excellent viewpoint into the aquatic habitats.

Streatham to Wimbledon Park

Boundaries Road **O** and continue ahead. At the bend, turn right along a passage **P** onto Wandsworth Common **7**, which is quite extensive but has been shattered by roads and railway into several shards. For a third time you encounter the Brighton Line, and march impertinently through the ticket office of Wandsworth Common Station **Q**. Follow the station approach road round to the left and cross at the lights over both St James's Drive and Bellevue Road, passing The Hope pub **R** *(cafés to your left)*. Take the furthest right of three tarmac paths onto the next part of Wandsworth Common, rejoining the railway line. You pass a large pond, which has a boardwalk and viewing platform at its far end.

At the footbridge **S** over the railway, keep ahead then straightaway fork left on the third path, heading for the right-hand end of a long brick wall (shared cycle track, keep right). The cream building to your right, the former Neal's Farmhouse **8**, now contains a café, toilets and a nature study centre run by the London Borough of Wandsworth. Those with energy to spare could try the trim trail that leads off to your left, on a circuit that brings you back to the footbridge. To continue, bear left between the fences then keep ahead, parallel to Dorlcote Road. Away to your right now is a yellow-brick building, whose pyramid-roofed tower rises above the trees. This vast Gothic edifice

is the Grade II-listed Royal Victoria Patriotic Building of 1858, built as an orphanage and recently restored for mixed use with residences, a community centre, workshops and a bar-restaurant.

Towards the end, bear left up a short grit path to the traffic lights at Trinity Road **T** *(buses)*. Cross at the lights and continue ahead beside the County Arms pub along Alma Terrace. Ahead loom the forbidding brick wall and buildings of Wandsworth Prison **9**, built in 1851 as the Surrey House of Correction. Former inmates include Oscar Wilde in 1895, imprisoned for homosexuality (you shortly pass a street called Wilde Place), and in 1963 the Great Train Robber Ronnie Biggs, until his notorious escape in 1965. In 1953, Derek Bentley was hanged here, wrongfully convicted of the murder of a policeman; the conviction was overturned in 1998.

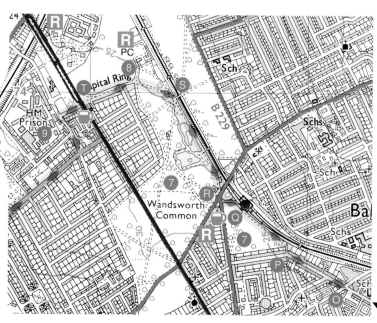

Turn left beside the prison along Heathfield Road **U**. At the mini-roundabout **V**, turn right into the long and straight Magdalen Road, which you follow for half a mile. Most of this road adjoins Wandsworth Cemetery **10**, which is open to the public. *You can if you prefer walk the length of the cemetery by entering at the main gate* **W** *and following the parallel path to leave by a kissing-gate* **X** *at the far end. However to avoid getting locked in you must check the closing times, which are shown at the entrance, or phone 020 8871 7820.* At A217 Garratt Lane **Y**, with Earlsfield Station **Z** to your right *(buses, several pubs and cafés).* Cross over then turn right under the railway bridge. Tucked quietly away along Thornsett Road on your left is the little Country House pub. At the traffic lights **AA** turn left along Penwith Road.

You shortly cross the River Wandle **11**, which flows through Mitcham to join the Thames at Wandsworth. It is one of the fastest-flowing rivers in the London area, and used to provide some of the best trout fishing in Britain and power for a host of watermills. This was one of London's most active industrial areas, and it must have been a nauseous place. Soap and chemical manure were produced nearby, while a fireworks factory consisted of wooden huts, set some distance apart so that an explosion in one was less likely to ignite another. The decline of industrial activity in recent years has allowed much of the Wandle to be turned into a nature reserve. This is more evident further south, but only a few hundred yards away to the left, at Trewint Street, a narrow band of greenery stretches almost unbroken for nearly 2 miles to Colliers Wood. The Wandle Trail, which you cross at Garratt Lane, accompanies the river for 11 miles from Waddon to Wandsworth.

Shortly turn left into Ravensbury Terrace **AB**, then bear right with the bend, passing the Haslemere Industrial Estate, into Haslemere Avenue **AC**, where you enter the London Borough of Merton. Cross Dawlish Avenue and Brooklands Avenue, keeping ahead into Mount Road. Take the next left, Lucien Road **AD**, and go through the gate **AE** at the end into Durnsford Road Recreation Ground **12**. Follow the tarmac path around a fenced play area, then turn sharp right to pass a school and playground, into Wellington Road **AF**. Turn left, then at the end, beside Field Court **AG**, turn right along a short footpath leading to Durnsford Road **AH** *(buses).*

Turn left to cross at the lights, towards the white-tiled, minaretted Wimbledon Mosque **13**, opened in 1977. Turn left along the far side for 150 yards, then turn right up Arthur Road **AI** just before The Woodman pub. In 250 yards you reach Wimbledon Park Station **AJ**, where Walk 5 finishes. *To continue on to Walk 6, stay on the right-hand side and keep ahead.*

The Wandle Valley

The Capital Ring flattens out as it crosses the valley of the Wandle, once one of the fastest-flowing rivers in the London area. Our route avoids much of the urban sprawl by crossing three large commons: Streatham, Tooting Bec and Wandsworth.

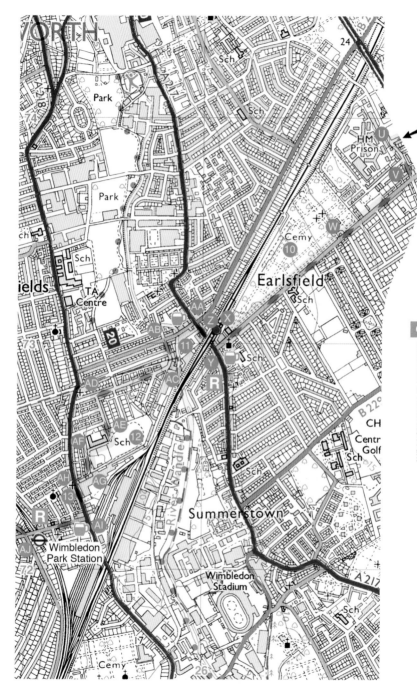

6 Wimbledon Park to Richmond

Distance 7.0 miles (11.3 km). Excludes link of 0.5 miles (0.8 km) to Richmond Station.

Public transport Walk 6 starts at Wimbledon Park Station, with buses 250 yards away in Durnsford Road. It finishes near Richmond Bridge, which has buses and riverboat services nearby and is half a mile from Richmond Station. There are links to bus stops at Kingston Vale. Wimbledon Park Station is in Travelcard Zone 3, Richmond Station is in Zone 4.

Surface and terrain The first 2 miles are on pavements or tarmac paths — level at first, then a fairly steep climb up to Putney Heath. Then the route is almost entirely on earth paths and tracks with some steep gradients nearly all the way to Richmond. The final stretch beside the Thames is on level tarmac.

Refreshments Wimbledon Park, Wimbledon Common, Pembroke Lodge, Petersham and Richmond.

Toilets Wimbledon Park, Wimbledon Common, Richmond Park, Petersham Park, Buccleuch Gardens and Richmond Station.

Signs Note that street signs in Petersham and Richmond have a black background instead of standard Capital Ring green, to meet local planning requirements.

Walk 6 starts in Arthur Road, SW19 opposite Wimbledon Park Station **A**, in the London Borough of Merton. *From the station exit, go over the zebra crossing then turn left.* Shortly turn right along Home Park Road, then in 200 yards turn right through a gate **B** into Wimbledon Park **1**, one of London's oldest recreational open spaces. It was formed towards the end of the 16th century from part of Wimbledon Common, and originally included the golf course and what is now the All England Lawn Tennis and Croquet Club. The supreme landscape designer Capability Brown redesigned the park in the mid-18th century, creating the lake.

Open Spaces
Many Capital Ring walkers rate this section the prettiest of the route, as it crosses three vast and delightful open spaces – Wimbledon Park, Wimbledon Common and Richmond Park – and conveniently passes their tea rooms.

Descend several flights totalling 34 steps, passing through a viewing platform, or there is ramped access to the right. At the bottom, turn left through a gate, then follow a tarmac path through a play area, forking left to leave it through another gate. *Over to your right, by tennis courts, are toilets and a chalet-style café.* Take the path up to Wimbledon Park Lake **2**, where you should see plenty of waterbirds and perhaps some sailing boats, while on your right are the pretty Waterfall Gardens **3** and a crazy-golf course. Follow the lakeside path to the sailing base **C** *(toilets)*. Turn right to the main sign, then bear left on a path that leads to and beside the fence of an athletics stadium **4**, the home of Hercules Wimbledon Athletic Club. As the fence ends, go slightly left across grass, heading for the park gates **D**.

(You can avoid the grass by going left then right on a tarmac path.)

Go out into Wimbledon Park Road and turn left beside the park, entering the London Borough of Wandsworth. To your left, across Wimbledon Park Golf Course, is another view of the lake.

For the next couple of miles you follow the boundary between Merton (to your left) and Wandsworth (to your right), switching back and forth between the two boroughs. In 350 yards you reach a major junction **E**. Ahead now and on the right is the All England Lawn Tennis and Croquet Club **5** with its tennis museum – this area is heaving with activity during Wimbledon fortnight at the end of June and beginning of July. Turn right across the road at the second refuge, then keep ahead along Bathgate Road.

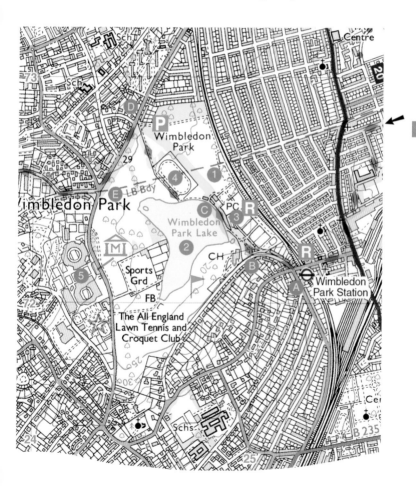

Wimbledon Park's lake, created by Capability Brown, is enlivened by sailing dinghies and waterbirds. Beyond the poplars lies the park's athletics stadium.

Wimbledon Common's unusual 19th-century hollow post mill rises above a museum devoted to windmills

In 175 yards, turn right into Queensmere Road **F**. To your left lie some practice tennis courts for the All England Club and the impressive Royal Close **6**, now converted into luxury apartments. It used to be Queensmere House, formerly a college, which was a prisoner-of-war camp for officers during World War II. Climb fairly steeply for 700 yards to the A219 Wimbledon Park Side **G** *(buses)*.

Turn right and cross at the traffic lights **H** onto wooded Putney Heath **7**. Keep ahead, then bear slightly left along a broad gravel track. Nearly all of the remainder of Walk 6 is on such tracks and paths, and may be muddy in places. At the end, you reach an open area near the famous windmill **8**. Cross a broad track and keep ahead on a path towards the mill, beside which are a museum and tearoom. You pass a stone which originally just marked the boundary between the parishes of Putney and Wimbledon, but now also separates the London Boroughs of Wandsworth and Merton. The windmill, built in 1817, is most unusual, being the only remaining example in Britain of a hollow post mill: the main body of the mill, with all its machinery, originally turned on a central post, through which a hole was bored for a drive shaft taking power to the machinery. This was replaced in 1893 by an iron bearing. Putney Heath and Wimbledon Common together form one of the largest public open spaces in Greater London. The route of the Capital Ring lies mostly on Putney Heath, peeping into Wimbledon Common **9** in the area around the windmill.

Keep ahead on a dirt path **I** between the tearoom and car park, passing toilets. Bear left past the clubhouse of the London Scottish Golf Club, whose red-lion coat of arms adorns the gables. You can easily identify its members, who are required to wear red tops while playing. At the end of the hedge and fence, just before the golf course, turn right down a broad dirt path, which descends fairly steeply for 250 yards to Queen's Mere **10**, formed in 1887 by damming a stream that feeds Beverley Brook. In Elizabeth Beresford's books, this was a favourite retreat of the Wombles, although its serene appearance is rather disturbed by the distant roar of the A3.

At the narrow end of the mere **J**, turn left up a rising earth track amid trees. At the top you must cross a golf fairway; watch out for rapidly

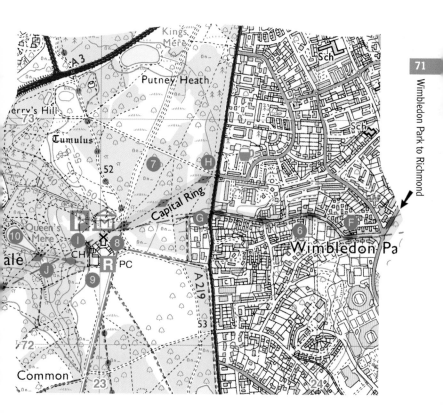

approaching golf balls. Continue along the track through more trees, then cross a second fairway; again, take care. Back amid the trees, take the left fork **K**, with a bench seat on your right, and follow it for 175 yards down to a track junction. Continue downhill to the next junction **L**. Ahead now, through the trees, are the circular, hedge-bound Memorial Gardens **11**, with a World War I memorial at its centre. Turn left along a broad and usually muddy track as it swings right. At a grassy and brambly triangle **M**, bear right on a narrower footpath, which soon joins tracks beside Beverley Brook **12**. Bear right, with the brook just to your left, to pass a wooden footbridge. The brook rises in Nonsuch Park near Cheam and

flows through New Malden and Richmond Park to the Thames at Putney. For the next half-mile the Capital Ring joins the Beverley Brook Walk, marked by its cerise and yellow waymarks.

In 350 yards turn left to cross a brick-walled footbridge **N** over the brook, with a pavilion to your right (*toilets*) which serves the pitches of several rugby football clubs. For the next 500 yards, the Capital Ring pays a very brief visit to the Royal Borough of Kingston-upon-Thames. Fork right towards a footbridge then cross the A3 Kingston Bypass (Robin Hood Way) **O** at surface level, using a two-stage light-controlled Pegasus crossing – so called as it is also used by horses (from

According to Elizab Beresford, Queen's Mere spot favoured by the Womb

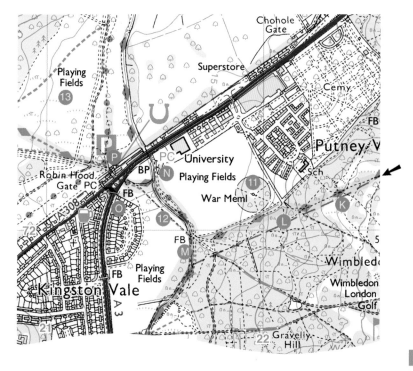

Pegasus, the winged horse). *(You can use the footbridge if preferred. Bus stops nearby.)* Keep ahead past the late-18th-century Stag Lodge Stables, and go through Robin Hood Gate **P** into Richmond Park **13**. *There are toilets on your left inside the gate (20p).* The rest of Walk 6 lies in the London Borough of Richmond-upon-Thames. For centuries, Richmond Park was used by England's hunting-mad royalty, and in 1637 was enclosed for their sole use by Charles I. The park is still owned by the Crown and managed by the Royal Parks Agency. It is now a national nature reserve and the largest urban park in Europe at around 2½ miles from side to side and top to bottom. Towards the centre, the view as far as you can see consists of woods, meadows and ponds. Richmond Park is

famous for its deer, of which the park has around 650. There are two kinds: red (the darker, larger ones) and fallow (the smaller, light-brown, dappled ones). It is worth quoting the park's warning notices: 'It is always dangerous to go close to the deer, but especially in May, June, July, September and October. Feeding or touching the deer is prohibited. Dogs must be kept under control and not be allowed to worry the deer. Dogs approaching too closely may be attacked.'

The roads inside Richmond Park are heavily used by traffic, so take care when you have to cross them. Bear half right across a car park to pass a black board with a car park map, then cross a road hump. Bear slightly right on a dirt path among widely

The Pen Ponds in Richmond Park, a haven for waterbirds, were created by damming a stream that feeds Beverley Brook.

spaced trees, crossing a sandy ride to reach a wide, open pasture. Follow the path as it climbs steadily, heading for the left end of Spankers Hill Wood. You join a track to cross the brow of the hill to a car park **Q** ahead, with a refreshment kiosk.

Keep ahead along a gravel track towards the distant Pen Ponds. Away to the right among trees is White Lodge **14**, built around 1727 and now the home of the

Royal Ballet's Lower School. Further on comes an area of tussock grass, where the park management is encouraging the ground nesting of birds such as skylarks, reed bunting, stonechat and meadow pipit – dogs should be kept on a lead here. You pass between the Pen Ponds **15**, usually surrounded by family groups observing the antics of waterbirds. These ponds, too, were formed by damming a stream that feeds

Beverley Brook. If it feels especially cold here on a winter's day, blame it on the topography: the Pen Ponds lie in a notorious frost hollow.

Though you may hear distant traffic on the park roads, and you are beneath a flight path to Heathrow Airport, this is a relatively peaceful area. Once past the ponds, keep going in the same direction, climbing a track through more tussock grass and bracken. Halfway up, you cross a broad track, then in a further 100 yards, shortly

before the brow, turn left along a level path past a bench **R**.

You come now to Sidmouth Wood **16**, named after Lord Sidmouth, who was responsible for planting most of the park's woodlands during the early 19th century. Follow the track by the fence **S** ahead. Except when trees are in full leaf, away to the left soon you should see Whiteash Pond and Whiteash Lodge, built in the mid-18th century and now a base for the Royal Parks Constabulary. As the track swings right, you pass Oak

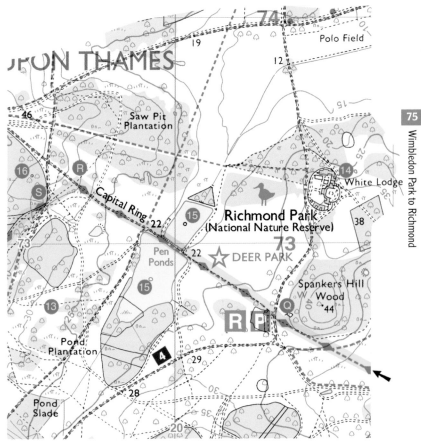

Lodge **17**, built in 1850 and now accommodating some of the park's management staff. Follow its tarmac drive ahead to the western park road **T**.

Cross the road carefully and keep ahead along a stony path for 75 yards, passing a pedestrians' gate **U** into Pembroke Lodge Gardens. *You can use this gate to avoid steps later ilf you wish to visit the cafeteria or the toilets and refreshments kiosk (beside the car park).*Go down steps and bear right, with a great view to your left. You are now in Petersham Park **18**, added to Richmond Park in 1843. It contains some beautiful trees, and deer can be seen too. Descend steps and follow the path parallel to the fence, passing another pedestrians' gate **V** into

the gardens before a bench. Pembroke Lodge **19** is close by up a steep flight of 65 steps. Originally the home of the park's molecatcher, in 1788 it was converted into an imposing residence for the Countess of Pembroke. During the 19th and early 20th centuries it was occupied by members of the aristocratic Russell family, and philosopher Bertrand spent his childhood here. Requisitioned for military use during World War II, it later became a rather grand cafeteria.

In a further 250 yards at another bench **W**, the Capital Ring bears half-left downhill, *but a short diversion is recommended to the right to see the King Henry's Mound **20**, reached through another gate into the gardens.*

Richmond Bridge has spanned the Thames for more than two centuries.

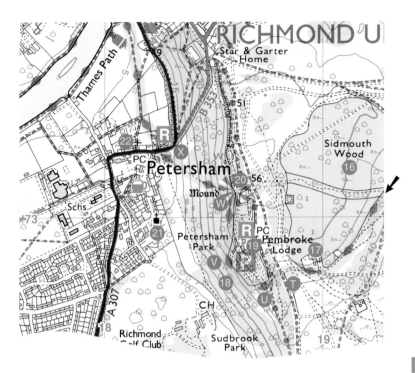

The mound is actually a prehistoric round barrow or burial mound, but has a sinister connection with Henry VIII. He is supposed to have stood here in 1536, looking out for a flare from the Tower of London which would confirm that Anne Boleyn had been executed, leaving him free to marry Lady Jane Seymour. The view is extensive, to the hills of Berkshire and Surrey. And, like Henry, you can look through a telescope, but now seeing the dome of St Paul's Cathedral on a clear day, nearly 10 miles (16 km) away, through a convenient gap in the trees.

As you descend towards Petersham village, the view across West London is dominated by the massive stands of 'Twickers' – Twickenham Rugby Ground. The eye-catching, romanesque red-brick building to your left, with campanile, was

All Saints' Church **21**. It was built in 1908 as a second church for Petersham, which at that time was expected to grow larger than it did. It has now been converted into a luxury home. The little white bell tower ahead, with wind vane, sits on top of Petersham's much older parish church of St Peter **22**, dating from the 13th century. Leave the park through Petersham Gate **X**; *there are toilets (20p) in the playground to your left*. The Fox and Duck pub lies 350 yards around to your left outside the gate. The gate occupies a gap in the 8-mile-long, 8-feet-high brick wall that almost surrounds Richmond Park and its adjoining territories. Local brickmakers must have made a killing out of this project in 1637 when the park was enclosed – by the author's estimate, over five million bricks would have been needed.

Cross the A307 Petersham Road *(buses)* at the pedestrian crossing towards the Dysart restaurant. The route continues opposite, along a fenced earth footpath, which twists and turns between sheds and St Peter's churchyard. Turn right along a driveway. *If you wish to visit the church, turn left. Hidden away in the churchyard, by the south wall, is the tomb of the 18th-century explorer Captain George Vancouver, a Petersham resident.*

At a bend **Y** in the drive, keep ahead along a footpath through Petersham Meadows **23**. Famously painted by Turner, and usually occupied by cattle, these fields are regularly flooded by the Thames with permission, as it were, from the local authority – this helps to maintain them in their natural state. Up to your right is the imposing Royal Star and Garter Building **24**, opened in 1924 as a retirement home for disabled ex-servicemen and women. They recently moved elsewhere and the building has been converted into private apartments. The smaller but no less grand building is the Petersham Hotel. Keep ahead at a barrier **Z**, gradually closing in on the riverside. Go through a swing gate and keep ahead through Buccleuch Gardens **AA**, *with toilets on your right.*

For the next 3 miles, the Capital Ring shares the route of the Thames Path National Trail, one of 15 such routes in England and Wales. Launched in 1996, it runs for 184 miles (295 km) from the source of the river near Cirencester in Gloucestershire, through Oxford, Reading, Windsor and central London to finish at the Thames Barrier. The Thames itself is 205 miles (330 km) in length, continuing to The Nore sandbank, between Southend and Sheerness, where it formally ceases to be an estuary and becomes open sea. Follow the broad, tarmac path beside the river, with handsome Richmond Bridge **25** ahead, opened in 1777. You pass three low stone arches forming the Grotto Gate into a subway under the road via 17 steps into Terrace Gardens, which has a café with toilets. Refreshment kiosks and some rather smart eating establishments line the path at Richmond Landing Stage. To your right lies the bustling town of Richmond **26**, named by King Henry VII after his estate in Yorkshire when he built his new palace here. At that time, it was just a small fishing village, which until then had been called Shene.

At Richmond Bridge **AB** *(buses)*, keep ahead along Richmond Riverside **27**, one of the most impressive stretches beside the Thames. Its terraced gardens and adjacent buildings, dating from the 17th and 19th centuries, were beautifully restored in the 1980s. The white-painted stone building ahead, now a wine bar, was originally the Waterworks Pump House and later served as a brewery. There are several small islands in the river here, the largest being Corporation Island. *The alternative route, avoiding steps at Richmond Lock (see Walk 7), starts up the ramps beside the gardens on Richmond Riverside. There are toilets inside the disabled entrance of the Old Town Hall, just past the top of these ramps.* Pass the old White Cross pub at the foot of Water Lane **AC**, then St Helena Pier – this area may be under water at high tide (times for Richmond can be checked online at www.tidetimes.org.uk, under 'View All Locations'). Soon after this, Walk 6 ends at Friars Lane **AD**. *Walk 7 continues ahead.*

Capital Ring link to Richmond Station (0.5 mile / 0.8 km). Turn right up Friars Lane, using the pavement on the right-hand side, angling around a car park. At the top, keep ahead across three roads, watching out for traffic from the right. Keep ahead along the left-hand gravel path across Richmond Green **AE**. At the end cross right then left across Duke Street **AF** and keep ahead along Little Green, passing Richmond Theatre. Continue over the railway bridge then immediately turn right along Old Station Passage **AG** to a road called The Quadrant (buses), with Richmond Station **AH** opposite (toilets).

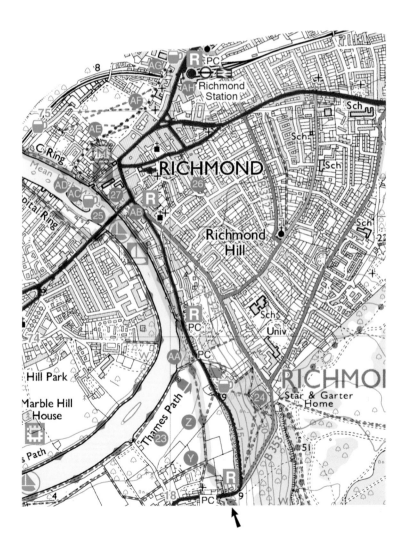

7 Richmond to Osterley Lock

Distance 4.0 miles (6.4 km). Excludes Capital Ring links 0.5 miles (0.8 km) from Richmond Station and 0.5 miles (0.8 km) to Boston Manor Station.

Public transport The start of Walk 7 is near Richmond Bridge, close to bus stops and Richmond Landing Stage (for riverboat services). Richmond Station is half a mile away. There is a link en route with Brentford Station. The finish at Osterley Lock is 500 yards from bus stops and half a mile from Boston Manor Station. All Stations on Walk 7 are in Travelcard Zone 4.

Surface and terrain Entirely on paving, tarmac or bonded gravel. Mostly level, but there are some short and fairly steep ascents along the Grand Union Canal towpath. There is a stepped footbridge over the Thames at Richmond Lock, which can be avoided on a Capital Ring alternative route. The Thames towpath north of Richmond is subject to flooding after heavy rain or at high tide. The link to Boston Manor Station includes a fairly long and steady ascent on a dirt track.

Refreshments Richmond, Old Isleworth, Syon Park, Brentford, Great West Road, Brentford Station and Boston Manor.

Toilets Richmond, Syon Park, Brentford Station and Boston Manor.

Signs Note that Capital Ring street signs in the London Borough of Richmond-upon-Thames have a black background instead of the standard Capital Ring green, to meet local planning requirements. Signs shared with the Thames Path also have a black background.

*Capital Ring link from Richmond Station (0.5 miles / 0.8 km). From the station's main exit **A**, turn left then cross the road (The Quadrant) at the pedestrian crossing. Keep ahead along Old Station Passage. Turn left over the railway, then walk along the left-hand pavement beside Little Green, passing Richmond Theatre. Cross Duke Street ahead, then immediately turn right across the road onto Richmond Green. Take the first gravel path, quarter-left, between the trees, aiming to the left of a little hut on the far side of the green **B**. Then cross the roads with care and continue in the same direction along the left-hand pavement of Friars Lane, which twists left then right past a car park to the River Thames **C**. You join the Capital Ring by turning right beside the river; go to point **C** on the next page.*

*The alternative route to avoid steps at Richmond Lock adds about 400 yards to the distance. It starts on Walk 6, shortly after passing under Richmond Bridge (point **AB** on page 78). At the far end of the terraces, turn right up zigzag ramps and keep ahead to Whittaker Avenue, passing the Museum of Richmond in the Old Town Hall. At the end, turn right along Hill Street, then in 100 yards turn right down Bridge Street to cross Richmond Bridge **D** over the Thames. On the far side, turn right along Willoughby Road **E**, later Ducks Walk, keeping ahead along a series of paved footpaths, shared with cyclists, for almost half a mile parallel with the Thames. At Richmond Railway Bridge **2** you rejoin the river, then keep ahead under Twickenham Bridge **3** into Ranelagh Drive. At the footbridge over Richmond Lock and Weir **F** keep ahead, joining the Capital Ring main route; go to point **F** on page 82.*

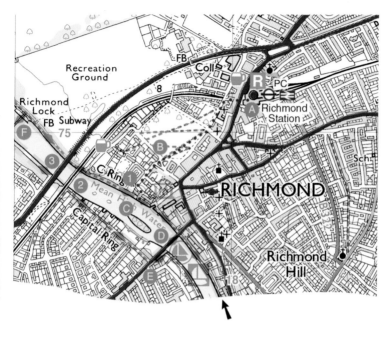

Walk 7 of the Capital Ring starts beside the River Thames at the foot of Friars Lane **C** in the London Borough of Richmond-upon-Thames. Still in company with the Thames Path National Trail (see Walk 6), which now occupies both banks of the river for most of its journey through London, you follow the towpath for the first half-mile. Continue along the riverside, here called Cholmondeley Walk, where the gardens to your right mark the site of the great Palace of Richmond **1**. Rebuilt in 1509 by Henry VII after a fire, this was the favourite residence of Elizabeth I, who died here. After the Tudor period, the palace fell out of favour and was partially destroyed by Cromwell's troops and left to crumble. Very little of the structure remains, but three impressive later buildings occupy the grounds. Queensberry House lies back a little, as does Trumpeter's House

with its impressive portico, now converted into rather grand apartments, on the site of the Middle Gate of the palace. Then, adjoining the towpath, comes the smaller Asgill House, in Palladian villa style, with its grand beech tree, on the site of the palace brewhouse.

Richmond's magnificent riverside terraces and adjacent buildings were restored in the 1980s.

Trumpeter's House occupies the site of the Middle Gate of Richmond Palace.

The White Swan pub lies 250 yards to your right along Old Palace Lane. Pass under Richmond Railway Bridge **2**, built in 1848 for the commuter line to Twickenham and Staines, then Twickenham Bridge **3** of 1933, carrying the A316 Great Chertsey Road. Ahead now are Richmond Lock and Weir, which you will shortly cross, while to your right is Old Deer Park **4**. This is part of the vast royal estate that once surrounded the Palace of Richmond, and included what is now Kew Gardens. Old Deer Park remains Crown property, but is nowadays shared between a public open space and a private sports ground. Prior to being shifted to Greenwich, the original meridian line passed through Kew Observatory, visible in the distance, which was built in 1769 for King George III. You can look along the meridian line to the observatory by squinting through a slotted metal post beside the towpath.

Richmond Lock and its accompanying weir and pretty cast-iron footbridges form a neat little operation that is rather pleasing to the eye, especially when river boats are passing through. Opened in 1894, it is actually a half-tide lock, by which boats can pass over the weir two hours either side of high tide. Climb the 36 steps up to the footbridge over Richmond Lock and Weir **5**. On the far side **F**, descend steps to the right, as the alternative route comes in from the left. (Note that the footbridge is closed at night, when Twickenham Bridge **3** provides an alternative.)

Keep beside the riverside along Ranelagh Drive to a board describing the River Crane Walk, which finishes here after accompanying that river from Feltham. Continue along the riverside footpath, which leads to gardens. Towards the end, behind a high wall here is the red-and-yellow-brick Gordon

House, with its clocktower, until recently part of the Twickenham Campus of Brunel University **6**. Gordon House dates from the 17th century. It started life as a rather grand private house, passed through various phases as a girls' school, a teacher training college, an institute of higher education, then part of Brunel University, but has now reverted to its origins as rather grand private apartments.

You reach the end of Railshead Road **G**, which used to serve a ferry. Beyond the houseboat mooring ahead lies Isleworth Ait **9** (see below) and an inaccessible stretch of river bank. It is hoped that a new riverside section will be available here eventually, but for the moment you must divert left along the road for a short distance to A3004

Richmond Road in St Margaret's *(buses)*. Turn right to cross the River Crane **7** and enter the London Borough of Hounslow.

Continue along Richmond Road for 400 yards, beside the wall of Nazareth House **8**, once a convent and care centre, and soon to be converted into more private apartments. At the junction with South Street in Old Isleworth *(buses)*, with a mini-roundabout **H** beside The Castle pub turn right along Lion Wharf Road. You rejoin the river beside Isleworth Ait **9**. Ait is a southern dialect word for island. A boat repair yard occupies the near bank, but this densely wooded island is a nature reserve with a mysterious air, being so close, yet only accessible by a narrow causeway at low tide.

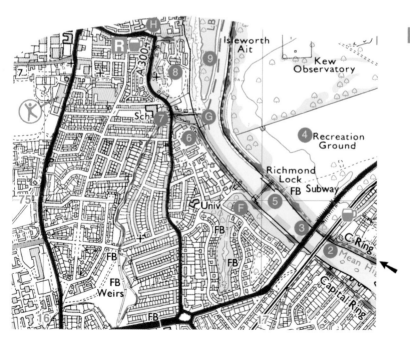

Turn left beside the river to the Town Wharf pub **I** and climb onto its veranda. You may have to thread your way between customers' chairs, but this is a public right of way. Cross a humped wooden footbridge, then at the 'electric pedestal crane' turn left beside the Duke of Northumberland's River **10**. Often abbreviated to Duke's River, this is an artificial channel of uncertain age, possibly dating from the 15th century. It was originally known as the Isleworth Mill Stream, providing water power, and received its current name when acquired by the Duke of Northumberland in 1605.

Another short inaccessible stretch of Thames river bank lies ahead. Turn right along Church Street **J** past the main sign, then cross over to follow the left-hand pavement. Number 43 Church Street on the left is Richard Reynolds House, named after a 16th-century chaplain of Syon Monastery. You rejoin

This 1920s scene shows the ferry that used to cross the Thames at Isleworth.

the riverside by the London Apprentice pub **11**, so called because members of the City Livery Companies rowed here to celebrate completion of their apprenticeships, and continue along the raised pavement beside All Saints **12**, the parish church of Isleworth. Isleworth lies in a very favourable riverside situation, a settlement since prehistoric times. The present All Saints Church was rebuilt in 1970 onto a 14th-century tower, after the 18th-century building was destroyed during World War II – not by enemy action but by vandals lighting a fire. Continue past the graveyard and round the bend. Peeping through the trees on your right is a pastel-pink building with a shallow green dome: this is The Pavilion, built at the start of the 19th century as a boathouse and picnic lodge for Syon Park. It lies next to The Ferry House, from which a ferry operated to the south bank for 400 years from Henry VIII's time until the start of World War II.

When you are opposite the gates **K** of Syon Park **13**, you can cross the road carefully with maximum visibility for traffic in both directions. Go through the gates to follow a gravel track to the right of the drive. Take care, as this is also a cycle route. Away to your left is a long lake **14**, which contains a trout fishery. Ahead, at either end of a ha-ha, lie twin lodges framing Syon House **15**. The Syon House and Park that you see today were created during the mid-18th century by the dream team of architect Robert Adam and landscape designer Capability Brown. The house (open to the public from March to October) is the London home of the Dukes of Northumberland, and is built on the

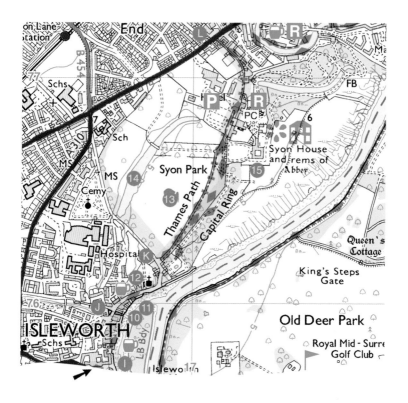

site of a convent, which was dissolved in 1539 during Henry VIII's purge. The nuns took the name from Mount Zion, overlooking Jerusalem. When Henry died in 1547, his coffin rested at Syon en route from London to Windsor – it is said that, in divine retribution, the coffin burst open and some of his body was eaten by dogs.

On rejoining the main drive, keep ahead past the entrance to Syon House to reach a garden centre, which contains The Refectory café and toilets. The great glass dome over to your right surmounts the Great Conservatory. Continue along the drive and past a car park into a walled lane, where you pass, on your right, the entrance to Snakes and

Ladders, a children's playground, and on your left some wings of the Hilton London Syon Park Hotel. Leave the park through Brent Lea Gate, continue to the A315 London Road **L** *(buses)*, then turn right to the pedestrian crossing. *For the facilities of Brentford town centre keep ahead along this side of the road.* Archaeological evidence indicates that Brentford was probably an important trading centre in prehistoric times, because of its location, obviously, by a ford over the River Brent, as well as one over the Thames. Here you part company with the Thames Path National Trail, which turns right beside the River Brent. To continue along the Capital Ring, cross at the lights then turn right along the far side.

There are many houseboat moorings along the River Thames, such as this one at Railshead opposite Isleworth Ait.

Cross Commerce Road **M** towards the main sign, then keep ahead past the Holiday Inn and bear left on to the towpath of the Grand Union Canal. For several miles, the Capital Ring now shares its route with the Grand Union Canal Walk and the Brent River Park Walk. Much of this part of the canal uses the River Brent, but in places they are separate, as here, and you see the river coming in ahead, while the canal goes off to the left through twin locks.

Pass the locks and cross a swing bridge. With the ultra-modern GSK House rising ahead, you walk beside Brentford Canal Basin **16**. The area on the far side of the footbridge has been redeveloped into a fashionable waterside district, called Brentford Lock, with apartments, restaurants, a piazza and a thriving mooring for canal boats. Some of the warehouses had canopies to provide shelter while loading and unloading goods, and you walk under one that survives, beside a little dock. There is a rather haunted atmosphere here, and you can imagine the ghosts of narrowboats and their crews, unloading cargo into the warehouse through its massive doors. The river and canal merge here for a while.

Pass under the railway line and continue to a second bridge **N**, which carries the A4 Great West Road through a hotbed of multinational companies. GSK House **17** is the worldwide headquarters of GlaxoSmithKline, one of the world's leading pharmaceutical and healthcare companies. It consists of four buildings linked by an enclosed 'street' with shops and restaurants for its 3000 staff.

Capital Ring link with Brentford Station (0.4 miles / 0.7 km). At the Great West Road **N**, climb the steps before the bridge then turn right along the road. (There is also a ramped access point 150 yards further along the towpath, past a wooden footbridge, after which you come back along Transport Avenue and turn left along the Great West Road.) Pass Great West Plaza and keep ahead to Boston Manor Road **O** (buses), which you cross, then turn right to Brentford Station **P**. If starting here, climb the steps to Boston Manor Road, turn right to the Great West Road **O** then turn left along it for 300 yards. Cross the canal bridge **N**, then descend the steps on the far side and turn left along the towpath.

Keep ahead under the bridge. The multi-coloured steel sculpture beside GSK House opposite, entitled *Athlete*, is by Allen Jones. An added feature for towpath walkers is the dramatic reflection of the skyscape in the sheer glass walls beyond. A wooden footbridge leads to Boston Manor Park and House. Continue past lonely Clitherow Lock **18**, named after the family that occupied the nearby Boston Manor House from 1670 to 1920. The M4 now approaches noisily, high up from the right, to follow the canal for a while. Yet, despite all the commercial activity in this area, the

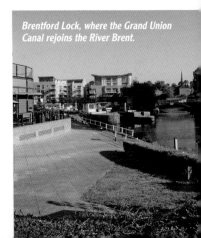

Brentford Lock, where the Grand Union Canal rejoins the River Brent.

immediate surroundings of the canal are predominantly green, and you might see a roosting grey heron or two.

Soon you change banks by crossing steeply humped Gallows Bridge **19**, a typical canal crossover bridge, made of iron in 1820. A high, battleship-grey bridge carries the Piccadilly Line, after which you pass under the M4 **Q** and into the London Borough of Ealing. The Capital Ring link to Boston Manor Station turns off here, but Walk 7 continues a further 200 yards to Osterley Lock **R**, crossing a footbridge onto an island formed by the separating river and canal. *Walk 8 continues along the towpath past Osterley Lock.*

Capital Ring link with Boston Manor Station and buses (0.5 miles / 0.8 km). Immediately after the M4 bridge Q, and before the foot bridge, turn right along the lower dirt path which bends left to climb fairly steeply through woodland to a path junction. Continue ahead to a drive and walk along it between houses to the A3002 Boston Road S, opposite a Harvester pub-restaurant and close to bus stops. Turn right for 350 yards to Boston Manor Station T (toilets).

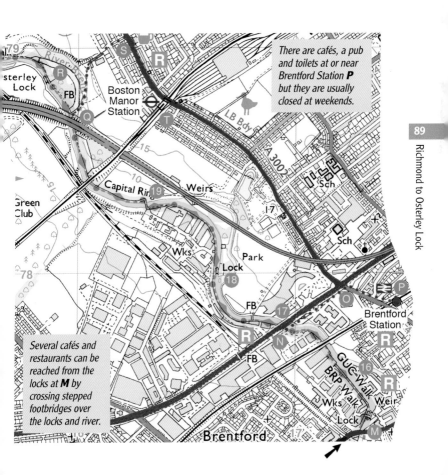

*There are cafés, a pub and toilets at or near Brentford Station **P** but they are usually closed at weekends.*

*Several cafés and restaurants can be reached from the locks at **M** by crossing stepped footbridges over the locks and river.*

8 Osterley Lock to Greenford

Distance 4.9 miles (7.9 km). Excludes Capital Ring links 0.5 miles (0.8 km) from Boston Manor Station and 0.2 miles (0.3 km) to Greenford Station.

Public transport The start of Walk 8 at Osterley Lock is 500 yards from bus stops on Boston Road and half a mile from Boston Manor Station. There is a Capital Ring link with Hanwell Station (no Sunday service), and the route passes South Greenford Station. The finish at Greenford is 300 yards from the station and bus stops. All Stations on this walk are in Travelcard Zone 4.

Surface and terrain The first and last miles are mostly on level tarmac, paving or bonded gravel, with some short, gentle ascents. The central section of 2 miles, from Hanwell Bridge to Greenford Bridge, is mostly on grass or earth paths, which may be muddy in places, or even under water after long periods of heavy rain. The link from Boston Manor Station is partly along a gently descending earth and gravel path.

Refreshments Boston Manor, Hanwell Bridge, Brent Lodge Park, Greenford Broadway, Westway Cross and Greenford Station.

Toilets Boston Manor Station, Brent Lodge Park and Greenford Bridge.

*Capital Ring link from Boston Manor Station (0.5 miles / 0.8 km). From Boston Manor Station (toilets) **A** turn left along Boston Road, crossing Wellmeadow Road, with bus stops nearby. In a further 250 yards, just past the Harvester pub-restaurant, turn left along a tarmac footpath **B**. Shortly cross Southdown Avenue and continue ahead along Wyke Gardens. Go ahead through a kissing-gate, then bear left along a path between fences. At a path junction, keep ahead to descend an earth then gravel path amid woodland. As you reach the M4 bridge **C** and the Grand Union Canal, turn right across a concrete bridge. Here you join the Capital Ring, briefly on Walk 7, to the official starting point of Walk 8.*

Walk 8 starts at Osterley Lock **D** in the London Borough of Ealing, where the Capital Ring still shares its route with the Grand Union Canal Walk and the Brent River Park Walk. As you continue along the canal towpath, the M4 mercifully swings away to the left. Though it can still be heard, the motorway passes out of sight, and there is a surprisingly rural feel to this area. To the right, the River Brent parts company with the canal again, flowing over a labyrinthine weir whose concertina design allows a greater flow of water in a confined space. Look out for a black-painted concrete slab beside the towpath commemorating the victory in 1959 of a British Waterways team in, of all things, a pile-driving competition.

The canal snakes between an industrial estate to the left and, to the right, Elthorne Waterside **1**, a former refuse tip that has

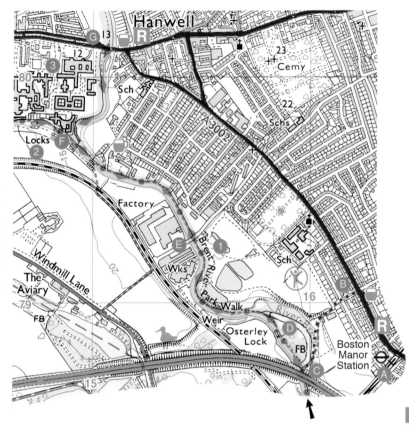

been grassed over and is now a nature conservation area. Pass under Trumpers Way **E**. A group of houses marks the start of Hanwell. The towpath crosses a bridge over the River Brent, which here makes its first rendezvous with the canal, while a pub known for its real ale, The Fox, lies just a short distance to the right. Ahead now lies the Hanwell Flight **2** of six locks, created in 1794, which raise the canal 53 feet in 600 yards. Between the first and second lock **F**, you leave the Grand Union Canal, which continues ahead to Birmingham, but continue with the

Brent River Park Walk. Soon after the first lock, turn right to follow a dirt path among trees beside the River Brent. This is known as FitzHerbert Walk, after Luke FitzHerbert (1937–2007), a leading light in the formation of the Brent River Park.

To your left now is the extensive Ealing Hospital **3**. In 400 yards, beside a small island formed by a side stream, you reach Hanwell Bridge **G** and A4020 Uxbridge Road *(buses)*. There has been a bridge at this point since the 14th century; the present one dates from 1762 and was widened in 1906.

At Hanwell, six locks raise the Grand Union Canal 53 feet in 600 yards.

You may be able to avoid crossing the road by passing under the old bridge, but as the path is often underwater you may need to cross the road at traffic lights to the right near the Viaduct pub and cafés. You continue on a sandy path along Brent Meadow, with the river below to your right and the striking Wharncliffe Viaduct **4** ahead. The viaduct carries the Great Western Railway over the Brent valley. It was named after Lord Wharncliffe, who steered the GWR Bill through the House of Lords, and whose coat of arms adorns the centre. As part of the GWR, the viaduct was designed by Isambard Kingdom Brunel and completed in 1838. At the end of the field, bear right to cross a footbridge over the river. Turn left under the viaduct and follow the path to a Capital Ring fingerpost **H** in a grass triangle in Churchfields Recreation Ground **5**, where the Capital Ring turns left.

Capital Ring link with Hanwell Station (0.3 miles/0.4 km, no Sunday service). *Keep ahead up a tarmac path, then turn right at the junction. Follow this path between fences to the road and keep ahead to a road junction beside a railway bridge **I**. Turn left along a road called Golden Manor, then in 75 yards turn right along Campbell Road. Follow this for 150 yards around a bend to Hanwell Station **J**. If starting here, from the main exit go ahead then left along Campbell Road. At the junction with Golden Manor, cross over then turn left. In 75 yards, just before the railway bridge **I**, turn right into Alwyne Road then cross over to follow a tarmac footpath between fences. In 150 yards, at the end of a row of houses, turn left down a narrower path towards the viaduct, then turn right by the fingerpost **H** to join the Capital Ring.*

Follow the gravel path, with the river to your left. To your right behind trees, on the hilltop site of the original Hanwell village, rises the spire of St Mary's Church **6**. Built in 1841, it was one of the earliest creations of eminent architect George Gilbert Scott. In 150 yards keep ahead beside a fence **K** into Brent Lodge Park, then turn left off the path to climb a short flight of shallow steps onto grass *(for café and toilets keep ahead past the steps and a pond)*. This used to be the grounds of a now-demolished mansion, home to the rectors of Hanwell.

The route officially follows the bends of the River Brent as it swings round a meadow on the west side of the park, though the river may be hidden when the trees are in full leaf. It can get very muddy and squelchy after heay rain, in which case keep to higher ground. On your right, behind a brick wall, is the Millennium Maze, planted in 2000 with

yew bushes, which could keep you occupied for a while. Further on, to your right past a zip-wire and playground, is an animal centre **7**. Soon after a green pipe over the river and a dip in the ground, you bend right towards the church. Descend steps on your left to a path junction **L**. *To visit the church, climb the gravel path to the right for 100 yards. Ahead lies Boles Meadow, a bird sanctuary where willow for basket-making is grown.*

Cross the bridge over the river, then turn right with a sports field to your left. Keep to the gravel path as it touches the river again and then crosses Brent Valley Golf Course **8**. Keep ahead, following a sheltered route among bushes – though you should still watch out for stray golf balls and allow golfers to finish their stroke when you pass a tee. After a stretch amid shrubbery, bear right by a low fence to cross a footbridge **M** over the river.

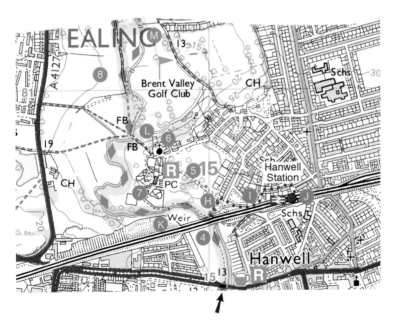

Turn left on grass and once more follow the east bank, briefly diverting around a reed-filled inlet. The riverside can get very wet and muddy here, so the route climbs steps up a bank onto a meadow, another grassed-over former refuse tip, prettily named Bittern's Field **9** – though you are unlikely to see such rare birds hereabouts. Follow the edge of the meadow for 500 yards, parallel with and above the river. At its end, bear left down to a grassy and often muddy track, still parallel with the river, to reach Greenford Bridge **N** on B455 Ruislip Road East. Turn left over the Brent and cross the road at a refuge. *For buses and cafés at Greenford Broadway keep ahead.*

Turn right along the far side and immediately bear left into Costons Lane using the left-hand pavement. *You now part company with the Brent River Park Walk, which turns right with the river, while the Capital Ring continues northwards.* Shortly after Costons Lane bears left, cross over and turn right along a track, which leads past a barrier **O** into Perivale Park **10**. Part of the riverside flood plain, its meadows are managed in traditional style to provide a wildlife haven.

Cross Costons Brook, then keep ahead past Perivale Park Golf Course. The path veers left to a park exit **P**. Do not go through; instead, turn right. At the athletics track, bear half-left to a small car park, then keep ahead across a side road onto the A40 Western Avenue **Q**. *To your right is South Greenford Station **R** on the little branch line from West Ealing to*

Greenford, a comparatively late addition to the railway network, opened in 1904 for the Great Western Railway.

Cross Western Avenue via the ramped footbridge. At the foot of the ramp on the far side, turn left along the side road, then shortly turn right along Cayton Road. At the end, by Northolt Rugby Football Club **S**, turn right along a paved footpath, which goes around Cayton Road Sports Ground **11**. Keep ahead at a path junction and continue to the far end. Turn right between posts into Bennetts Avenue **T** and follow it past Downing Drive, bearing left to reach A4127 Greenford Road **U**. Turn right under the viaduct and railway bridge, which carry the Central Line's West Ruislip branch.

Walk 8 ends at the junction with Rockware Avenue **V**, named after the great glassware manufacturers, now moved elsewhere, who dominated this area for many decades. To your right is the Westway Cross Shopping Park **12**. *If continuing on to Walk 9, keep ahead across Rockware Avenue at the traffic lights.*

> *Capital Ring link to Greenford Station (0.2 miles / 0.3 km). Turn left across Greenford Road at the traffic lights and go ahead along the HGV-infested Rockware Avenue, passing bus stops. At the end, opposite The Railway pub, turn left along Oldfield Lane, passing under the bridge, to find the station entrance **W** on your right (café nearby).*

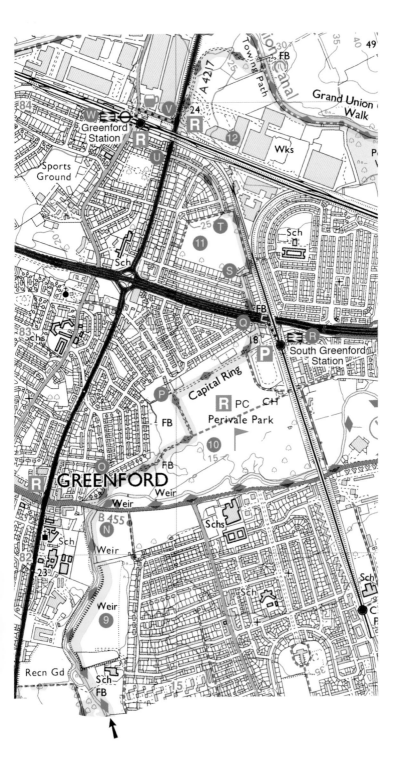

9 Greenford to South Kenton

Distance 5.5 miles (8.8 km). Excludes Capital Ring link of 0.2 miles (0.3 km) from Greenford Station.

Public transport The start of Walk 9 is 300 yards from Greenford Station and its bus stops. The route passes Sudbury Hill and Sudbury Hill Harrow Stations (Monday–Friday only), and there are Capital Ring links with Harrow-on-the-Hill and Northwick Park Stations. It finishes at South Kenton Station, with a bus stop nearby. All stations on this walk are in Travelcard Zone 4 except Harrow-on-the-Hill which is in Zone 5.

Surface and terrain This is one of the hilliest parts of the Capital Ring. A substantial amount is on uneven ground or grass, which may be muddy or wet after heavy rain, and there is one stile to climb over. There are two long and quite steep ascents and descents, over Horsenden Hill (with several long flights of steps) and through Harrow-on-the-Hill.

Refreshments Westway Cross, Horsenden Hill, Sudbury Hill, Harrow-on-the-Hill, Northwick Park and South Kenton.

Toilets Westway Cross, Horsenden Hill Visitor Centre, Sudbury Hill Station and Northwick Park Station.

A narrowboat on the Grand Union Canal near Paradise Fields Wetlands.

Walk 9 starts by crossing Rockware Avenue **B** at its junction with Greenford Road, in the London Borough of Ealing. Keep ahead past Westway Cross Shopping Park along a footpath/cycle track (keep left), with Greenford Road on your left and a car park and a McDonald's on your right. The track dips into a subway and emerges in a nature reserve called Paradise Fields **1**, where dogs must be kept on a lead. Converted from the former Greenford Golf Course, it contains several ponds and provides a good habitat for wildlife – lapwing have bred here recently. You pass a pond with

a viewing platform, then bear right on a bonded-gravel path across a meadow, with the West Ruislip branch of the Central Line away to your right.

The path soon rises to a footbridge **C**; do not cross it; instead bear left down a slope to be reunited with the Grand Union Canal – this time the branch from Paddington Basin. Go through a gate then turn right under a bridge. Follow the towpath for half a mile (beware cycles) as the canal swings back and forth, now with Horsenden Hill to your left, which you will soon be climbing. Further on, the trees of Perivale Wood Local Nature Reserve **2** lie to your right. A blank warehouse wall appears on the far bank, then you reach the old humped Ballot Box Bridge **D** at Horsenden Lane North. Pass under it, then in 20 yards turn sharp right up four steps to the road. *Perivale Station **E** is 600 yards to the left here, but with no official Capital Ring link.* Turn right and cross over the footbridge.

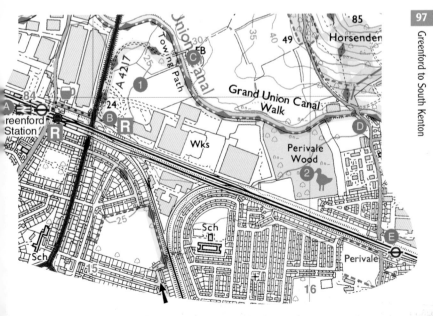

*An interesting alternative route here takes you past a café, visitor centre and toilets (though the café was closed for refurbishment in early 2016). For this, immediately after the bridge **D** turn right along a drive, then in 50 yards right again to follow a path beside the canal and past some imaginative wooden sculptures. In 150 yards turn left through the car park and keep ahead to a group of buildings **3**, where the café, toilets and visitor centre are located. The building to the left, originally a farmhouse, used to accommodate the Horsenden Hill ranger team, but it suffers from subsidence and they have moved elsewhere. Ascend steps to the right of the farmhouse to go through a gate. Keep ahead through another gate, beneath a carved wooden archway and over a crossing path to a T-junction. Turn left beside a wire fence and small meadow to enter woodland. In 50 yards go through a gate then bear right with the main path to reach another meadow. At its end, keep ahead over a crossing path to the next junction **F**, where the main route comes up from the left, and you turn right. Skip the next paragraph.*

The main route continues along the lane. In 40 yards, turn right past a barrier, then immediately leave the tarmac path on a dirt path bearing half-right into woodland. This climbs steeply on steps to pass through a gate into the first of several meadows. Keep ahead up to a path junction by more trees **F**. The alternative route comes in from the right here, and you keep ahead up more steps to another meadow with a fine view to your left.

The large skipper butterfly is a common sight in London's woods and grasslands.

Continue through a gate, then between bushes. This leads to a grassy terrace covering a reservoir. In 100 yards turn right, steeply up yet more steps, to the broad, grassy summit of Horsenden Hill **4**. This is one of the best natural viewpoints in Greater London. Another reservoir lies underneath, though this one is disused. Over to your right is a 'trig point' (concrete cairn), which marks the actual summit at altitude 260 feet (80 metres). Trig is short for triangulation: these structures were once used by the Ordnance Survey for measurements, but have been replaced by satellite data.

Keep ahead on a broad, gently descending grass track. Shortly fork left on a concrete path, dropping more steeply into Horsenden Wood **5**. In 20 yards immediately after a plank bridge, bear right on a dirt path down to a tarmac path. Turn right for 60 yards, then turn left along an earth path that runs parallel to garden fences to your right. This leads to a path junction at the end of Whitton Drive **G**. *Sudbury Town Station **H**, half a mile away, can* be reached by turning right along this road, but there is no official Capital Ring link. Turn sharp left along a tarmac path, with trees to your left and grass to your right, and follow it for 400 yards back to Horsenden Lane North **I** at the Ballot Box pub.

Turn right along the pavement, opposite a parade of shops, crossing Robin Hood Way and Drew Gardens. At the next junction **J**, where Horsenden Lane North bears left, the Capital Ring goes ahead into Melville Avenue. All Hallows Church

6, with its substantial brick tower, was built during World War II. Cross over at the refuge and continue in the same direction, now along the left-hand side. Cross Cambridge Avenue to reach A4090 Whitton Avenue East **K** (buses). Turn left to cross at the traffic lights **L**, then turn right for 20 yards and left up Ridding Lane. At the end, at Ridding Lane Open Space, bear left along a broad tarmac footpath. You rejoin A4127 Greenford Road **M**, turning right over the Piccadilly line into the London Borough of Harrow.

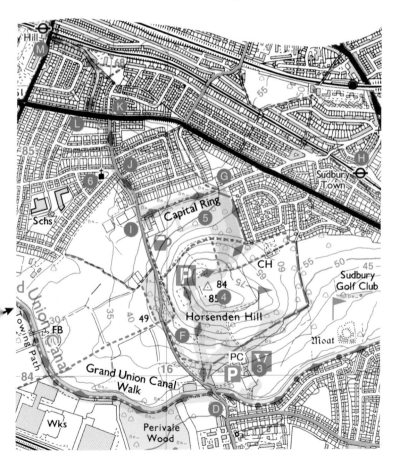

Greenford to South Kenton

Cross at the lights by Sudbury Hill Station **N** *(toilets)*, then turn right past a parade of shops and a café, and after 200 yards you reach Sudbury Hill Harrow Station (no service at weekends). In 30 yards, opposite the Rising Sun pub, turn left along South Vale **O**, keeping to the left-hand side for 300 yards. Up to your right, beyond a sports ground, the eye-catching mansion **7** was built around 1820 as Sudbury Hill House.

From 1929 to 1977 it was the sanatorium of Harrow School. The building was gutted by fire in 1980; it has since been absorbed into a residential development, incorporating part of the original façade. Where the road turns left as Wood End Road **P**, cross with great care, as traffic approaches quite fast. You should position yourself at the bend, where you can see and be seen by traffic approaching both ways.

Turn right up a stony historic track called Green Lane (known locally as Piggy Lane), which climbs steeply among trees, with houses to your left and a field to your right. During the 19th century, this was part of the road linking Harrow with Greenford. At the top, cross South Hill Avenue **Q** and keep ahead up the left-hand pavement of A4005 Sudbury Hill *(buses)*. This is Harrow-on-the-Hill, whose substantial houses reflect a long-standing prosperity. Once again the background of the Capital Ring signs turns black, in case the usual green upsets the delicate balance of the surrounding colours. At the top, where Sudbury Hill becomes London Road, and just before the junction with Mount Park Avenue **R**, cross carefully at the refuge and continue in the same direction along the right-hand pavement. Where the main road bends left **S**, keep ahead, still in London Road, to the little green **T** at the centre of the old village. At an altitude of 350 feet (105 metres), you are now at one of the highest points of the Capital Ring. And at 10 miles (16 km) from Charing Cross, this is as far from the centre as the Capital Ring gets. The hill, though compact, is isolated and can be seen for miles. It is thought to have been a place of pagan worship in prehistoric times, and the Saxon origin of the name Harrow means 'sacred grove'. Here, in 1094, the Normans built one of their earliest English churches, St Mary's **10**, which still stands, though much altered. Its spire, one of the highest points in North London, identifies the hill from afar.

Harrow

The Capital Ring reaches its furthest point from Central London as it crosses Harrow Hill, weaving between the red-brick buildings of the world-renowned public school where Sir Winston Churchill was educated. Then, crossing the school's playing fields, you can look back to see a classic view of the school on the hill above.

The white building on the far side of the green was until recently the King's Head Hotel **8**. It claimed to date from 1535 and to have been one of the places where Henry VIII courted Anne Boleyn, but the earliest documentary reference is in 1706. Continue past the green along the High Street and bus stop **U**. There are several cafés along here and West Street (leading sharp left behind a railing) descends in 150 yards to The Castle pub. You are now among the scattered, mainly red-brick buildings of

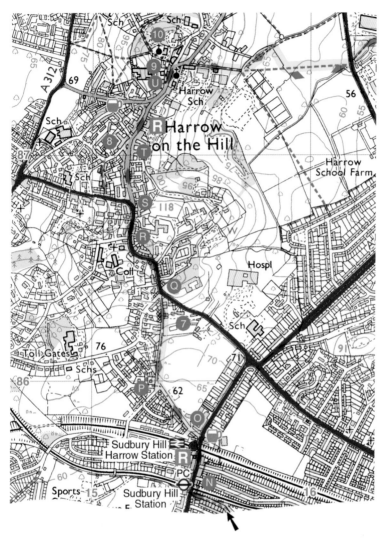

Harrow School **9**. Founded in 1572, it started with just one pupil, but its reputation grew steadily, and from the early 19th century the school was educating future statesmen such as Winston Churchill and Pandit Nehru, and great writers such as Byron and Trollope. Ahead lies the flint-dressed school chapel, consecrated in 1857,

with the chapel-like Vaughan Library of 1863 set back just before it. Up to your left in Church Hill, the red-brick building with a clocktower is the original school, dating from 1615. Beyond that rises the spire of St Mary's **10**, whose set of ten bells may accompany you through Harrow at times of services and celebration.

The Capital Ring continues along the High Street, opposite the school's Speech Room **Y** of 1877, described by Pevsner as being of partly Sicilian Gothic style. Bear right down Peterborough Road, then shortly turn right into the aptly named Football Lane **Z**, beside the Museum of Harrow Life (open selected Sunday afternoons in term time). This leads steeply down to Harrow School's playing fields. On the way you pass its Music School **11** of 1890, which bears the white-lion coat of arms of John Lyon, the local farmer who founded Harrow School. In the private car park at the bottom a signpost points ahead to Watford Road, and you may follow this if you wish, but as this direct right of way crosses sports pitches which may be in use, and may not be easy to follow, Harrow School has agreed a diversion. In the car park **AA**, turn left beside a tarmac drive for 200 yards, then turn right to follow a tree-lined track **AB**. On reaching a fingerpost among football pitches **AC**, turn left across grass – but don't miss the classic view back to the school on the hill. Coming to the corner of the playing field, follow a path ahead to cross a stile – the only one on the whole Capital Ring – onto A404 Watford Road **AD**. Go over the pedestrian crossing – 200 yards to your right is the Northwick Park Playgolf Centre, where Capital Ring walkers are welcome to use the refreshment and toilet facilities.

Now in the London Borough of Brent, follow the stony Ducker Path into a wood. It takes its name from the former outdoor swimming pool of Harrow School, where Sir Winston Churchill swam as a boy. The path bears right, beside the buildings of Northwick Park Hospital **12**. Pass through a gate then keep ahead beside a golf course on an uneven and sometimes muddy path to reach Northwick Park Playing Fields **13**. Turn right along the tarmac Proyer's Path **AE**.

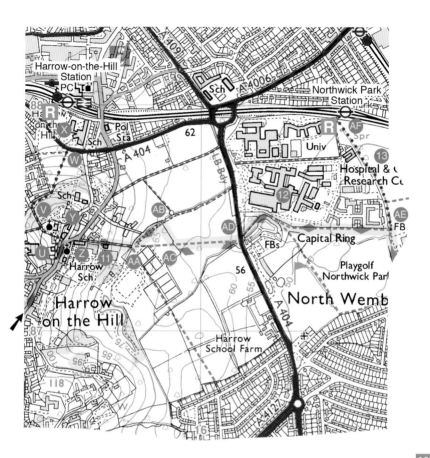

Capital Ring link with Northwick Park Station

*(0.4 miles / 0.6 km). At the path junction, turn left along Proyer's Path for 600 yards, passing the hospital and a University of Westminster building (café) to the entrance of Northwick Park Station **AF** (toilets). If starting here, from the ticket barriers turn left, directly into the park. Take the first path to the left, keeping a tall chimney to your right, and follow it for 600 yards, passing the end of the hospital fence **AE**, where you join the Capital Ring.*

The original building of Harrow School dates from 1615 and was enlarged in 1820.

Keep ahead through a car park, with a pavilion over to your left, and walk on grass to the left of its approach road. Just before the park exit **AG**, turn left, still on grass, to follow the park edge towards the railway, which is the West Coast Main Line **14** from Euston to the North West and Scotland, with the Bakerloo Line alongside. This section into Hertfordshire was one of the earliest railway lines in Britain, opened in 1837. It was extended to Birmingham in 1838 and Glasgow in 1848, becoming the famous LMS (London Midland and Scottish Railway) in 1923. Shortly before the railway, turn right into Nathans Road **AH**, then in 40 yards turn left into a cul-de-sac (The Link),

Harrow School Farm
The route passes close to this 60-acre farm, home to a herd of Longhorn cattle and flock of Shetland sheep.

which leads to the subway of South Kenton Station **AI**, the end of Walk 9. The ticket office and platforms are up 30 steps to the right. *Walk 10 continues through the subway.*

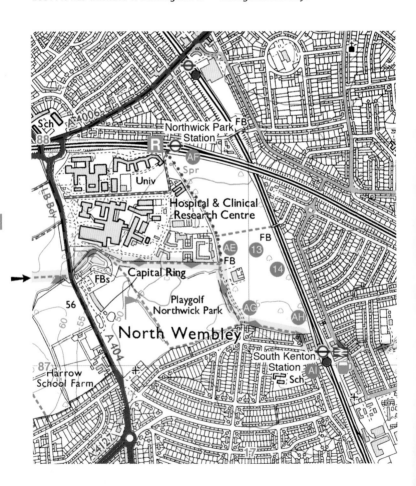

One of the highest points in North London, the spire of St Mary's in Harrow-on-the-Hill can be seen from miles around.

Distance 6.2 miles (10.0 km). Excludes Capital Ring link of 0.4 miles (0.7 km) to Hendon Central Station.

Public transport The start of Walk 10 is at South Kenton Station, with bus stops nearby. The route passes Preston Road Station, and there are links with Wembley Park and Hendon Stations. The finish in Hendon Park is just under half a mile from Hendon Central Station and buses. All stations on this walk are in Travelcard Zone 4, but Hendon and Hendon Central Stations are in both Zones 3 and 4.

Surface and terrain Mostly fairly level on tarmac, paving or bonded gravel, but the 2-mile central section through Fryent Country Park is on uneven or grassy paths, steep in places, which may be wet or muddy. Footbridge (23 steps) near finish.

Refreshments South Kenton, Preston Road, near Brent Reservoir, West Hendon Broadway and Hendon Central.

Toilets Preston Road Station and near Brent Reservoir.

The pond at the summit of Barn Hill was created by the landscape designer Humphry Repton. early summer an army of tiny frogs emerge

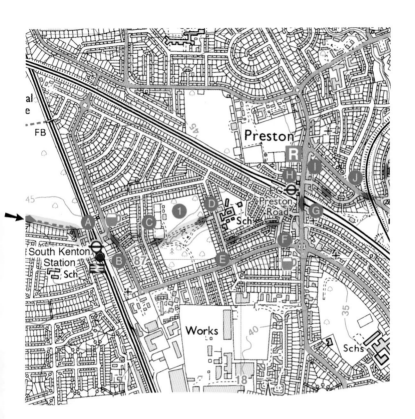

Walk 10 starts in the subway **A** under South Kenton Station, in the London Borough of Brent. From the platform, turn right at the foot of the steps out of the subway, then jink right and left past The Windermere pub. Cross Windermere Avenue *(buses)* and turn right, then in 70 yards turn left into Allonby Gardens **B**. At the end, go half-right along an alleyway leading to Montpelier Rise **C**. Cross over and turn right, then in 50 yards turn left through a gate into Preston Park **1**.

Go straight ahead through the park to College Road **D**, then cross over and turn right, past Preston Park Primary School. In 125 yards, turn left along Glendale Gardens **E**. At the end, turn left into Longfield Avenue **F**, cross Grasmere Avenue at the end, then turn right up to the busy Preston Road **G**, *where The Preston pub lies 200 yards to your right.* Turn left past Preston Road Station *(toilets on platform)* **H** and bus stops. Cross at the lights, turn left then right into Uxendon Crescent **I**; Uxendon is the name of the farm and hamlet that once occupied this area. At the end, turn right along The Avenue **J** and cross over at the refuge. Continue under the railway bridge, which carries the Jubilee Line to Stanmore. Over to the right is the Parish Church of the Ascension with its little stone-domed tower **2**.

Bear left up West Hill **K** at the grass patch, crossing Wealdstone Brook, which flows into the River Brent. In 60 yards turn left along Uxendon Hill and follow it round for 350 yards to turn left along a track between numbers 79 and 81 **L**. This leads into Fryent Country Park **3**, where for the next couple of miles you will be walking on grass or earth paths, which may be wet and muddy, and climbing quite steeply in places. However, the surroundings and views are well worth the effort. Fryent Country Park is a large nature reserve encompassing two high points, Barn Hill and Gotfords Hill, and a huge swathe of countryside where natural features are preserved as they have been for centuries. The park is divided into two by Fryent Way, with woodland dominating the western part and open grassland the east.

Keep ahead among trees and bushes, with the Jubilee Line to your left. On reaching a large meadow, stay beside the railway for 100 yards to a footbridge **M**, then turn right uphill to the far corner of the meadow. Keep ahead into the wood and follow the main broad earth path all the way to the pond at the top of Barn Hill **4**. Follow the path along the right-hand side of the pond and go on a few yards to a white trig point **N**, which marks the summit. At an altitude of 282 feet (85 metres), Barn Hill has long been a favoured viewpoint. You should have a fine view across West London, with Wembley Stadium beneath its spectacular 133-metre-high arch. On a clear day you should see the North Downs in the distance.

*Capital Ring link with Wembley Park Station (0.7 miles / 1.2 km). At the trig point **N**, turn left down a broad grassy track to a small car park and information board. Keep ahead along the road, also called Barn Hill, following the left-hand pavement all the way down to A4088 Forty Lane **O**. Cross at the lights near The Torch pub and cafés, turning right and left to continue in the same direction along the right-hand side of Bridge Road for 300 yards to Wembley Park Station **P**. If starting from here, at the barriers turn left then left again for 300 yards along Bridge Road to Forty Lane **O**. Turn right then left across the lights and continue in the same direction up the right-hand side of Barn Hill all the way to the top. Go past the information board, then bear half-left up a broad grassy track to the white trig point **N**.*

From the trig point, return to the pond and follow the path on its right-hand side. You do not quite complete the circuit: at the far end, 30 yards away from the path you came up by, keep ahead down a steep path, taking care over some exposed roots. Go all the way down, ignoring two crossing paths. You come to a field at the bottom **Q**, where there is a good view northwards over western Kingsbury. Turn right along a path through the trees, with the field to your left. In 250 yards you reach an intersection between fields, where a signpost reveals that the crossing track is called Eldestrete **R**. It is thought that this ancient road dates from pre-Roman times and was used by pilgrims to St Alban's shrine. *If you need to get to Kingsbury Station **S** (0.8 miles / 1.3 km off route), you can follow Eldestrete to the left, continuing along Fryent Way, though this is not an official Capital Ring link.*

Fryent Country Park

One of the least known but most delightful parts of the Capital Ring, Fryent Country Park passes through wooded hillside, around a pond with a magnificent view, and across fields that are still used for haymaking.

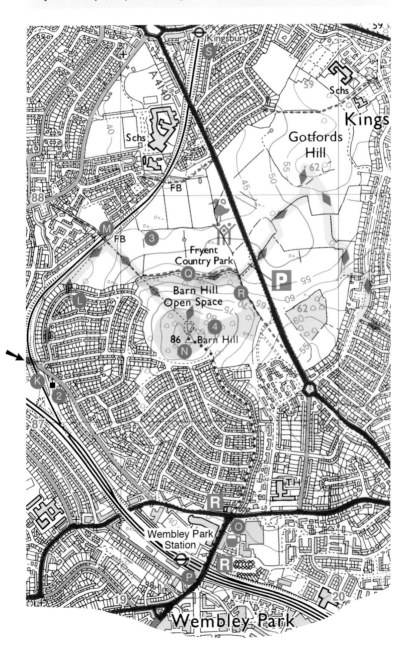

The route continues half-left across grass, passing park information boards, into a small car park. At the exit, keep left of a gate on to A4140 Fryent Way **T**. Cross at the lights, turn right to a layby then left over a grassy bank. The character of the country park now changes completely, as you pass through meadows of varying sizes. The livestock that used to graze them has gone, and the grass is mown annually to provide fodder for horses at local stables. In summer the meadows come alive with thousands of butterflies.

Bear half-left beside a hedgerow, then keep ahead past a small pond into the next field. Follow the hedgerow along the left-hand side of this large field as it bends right. At the far left-hand corner, turn left through a gap in the hedge and keep ahead across the next small field, now with the hedgerow on your right. Carry on through another gap, keep ahead to the top, then turn right to the Capital Ring main sign at the summit **U**. From the rounded summit of

Gotfords Hill, you have a magnificent 360-degree panorama over much of North and North-west London. To the west, you should be able to see Harrow on-the-Hill, from Walk 9, with the spire of St Mary's Church.

Turn right along a mown path to the field corner, a little to the right of a tall black Italian poplar tree. Go through a gap and keep ahead, with the paddock fence of Bush Farm Stables just to your left and the Wembley arch away to the right. At the end of the field, you cross plank bridge to find yourself facing a hedge end **V**. Turn right then immediately left into the next field keeping close to the hedgerow, now on your left, in this field, and the next. At the end, cross a ditch into the next field turn left and follow the hedgerow. In 5 yards, with houses ahead, turn right, still in the same field with the hedgerow to your left. At the top, pass a gap, then at a path junction beside a copse, turn left to head for a brick wall. Go to the left of it along a grass track between fences, and pass between posts to arrive on Salmon Street **W**, in a residential part of eastern Kingsbury.

Cross Salmon Street, then turn right along the pavement. Cross Mallard Way then in 150 yards, as the road swings right, turn left along Lavender Avenue **X**. Soon after this road veers left, turn right down Holden Avenue **Y**. At the end, cross Dunster Drive **Z** and turn left to B454 Church Lane **AA**. Turn right for 50 yards, then cross over at the refuge by Wells Drive, continuing along the opposite side of Church Lane. Just before the bend, you pass the 'new' St Andrew's Church **5** on your left, with it

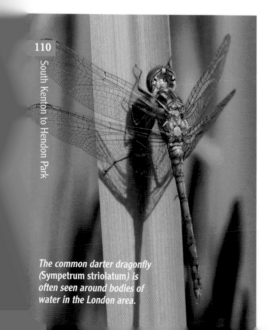

The common darter dragonfly (Sympetrum striolatum) is often seen around bodies of water in the London area.

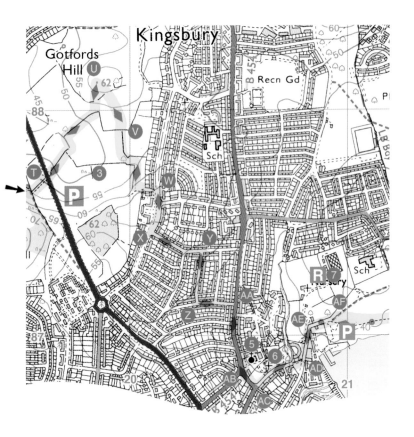

tall stone spire. The church was actually built in 1847 in Wells Street, Marylebone, and was well known in its day for musical performances. After lying redundant for some years, between 1931 and 1933 it was moved here, stone by stone, to become the parish church of Kingsbury, adjacent to and replacing the old St Andrew's. The interior is quite striking, giving the impression of a small cathedral.

Bear left into Old Church Lane **AB**, passing an overgrown cemetery. At the next bend **AC**, turn left, along Old St Andrew's Mansions, cross over and turn left along the pavement behind a grass bank, with old St Andrew's **6** to your left. Standing among shrubs and beautiful yew trees, in what is now a nature reserve, it has been restored to become a Romanian Orthodox Church.

Soon after a right-hand bend, you cross Birchen Close and pass a barrier to reach a T-junction. Turn left along Birchen Grove **AD**, then turn right at a bend **AE**. *There are toilets 300 yards ahead through the gate at the Birchen Grove Garden Centre 7, which also has a café.* At the end of the road **AF**, pass a car park to your right. Go half-right past a gate

along a tarmac shared cycle track with a black interpretative kiosk over to your right, then Brent Reservoir **8** shimmers into view. It is known locally as the Welsh Harp, after a pub that used to stand nearby. Built in 1835 to supply water to the Regent's Canal, it is one of the largest sheets of water in Greater London, at nearly a mile in length and a quarter of a mile across at its widest point. The reservoir and its surroundings are a naturalists' paradise: fauna recorded over the years include nearly 250 species of bird and 200 species of moth. For a while, this was one of London's leading visitor attractions, with its own railway station nearby, though this closed in 1903, and the rowing events of the 1948 Olympic Games were held here.

The level track runs along the gently sloping parkland on the north bank of the reservoir. Beyond the reservoir you can see and hear the roar of traffic on the North Circular road, though this is reduced a little by trees. In 500 yards, by a notice board, you enter the London Borough of Barnet. Occasional gunshots may disturb the tranquility, but not to worry – they are under supervision of the Hendon Rifle Club behind a wall away to your left. Pass the wooden cabins, slipway and pontoons of the Phoenix Outdoor Centre. Approaching the end, a viewing platform appears on your right, overlooking the northward spur of the reservoir **9**, formed from the Silk Stream. Keep on to Cool Oak Lane **AG** and cross over carefully. The detached part of the reservoir beyond has the appearance of a seaside creek, though the impression may be rather compromised by the construction of Hendon Waterside, a large residential estate.

Turn right across the narrow bridge, but as this has no pavement you must await your turn: press the pedestrians' button and wait for the green walking man to light up. Continue along the left-hand side of Cool Oak Lane for 300 yards to reach A5 West Hendon Broadway **AH** *(buses)*. Cross at the lights and turn left for 30 yards to reach the junction with Park Road **AI**, where the Capital Ring turns right. The dead-straight A5 is a continuation of Watling Street, the old Roman road that you encountered on Walk 1, which headed from Londinium through Verulamium (St Albans) to the fortress of Viroconium (Wroxeter) on the Welsh border.

Capital Ring link to Hendon Station *(0.3 miles / 0.5 km). At Park Road **AI**, keep ahead along West Hendon Broadway for 200 yards. At the next traffic lights, turn right up Station Road **AJ** and follow it around to the zebra crossing by Hendon Station **AK**, near the Midland Pub. If starting here, from the station exit turn right up to Station Road and go over the zebra crossing. Turn right down to the traffic lights, then turn left along West Hendon Broadway **AJ** for 200 yards to Park Road **AI**, where you cross over and turn left.*

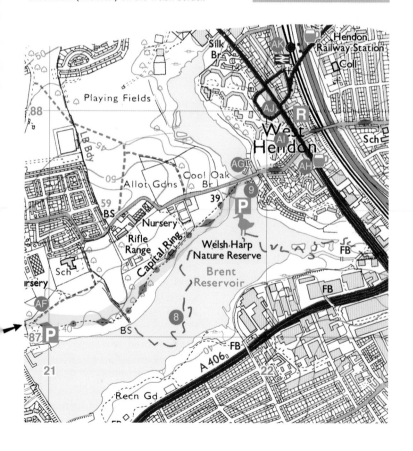

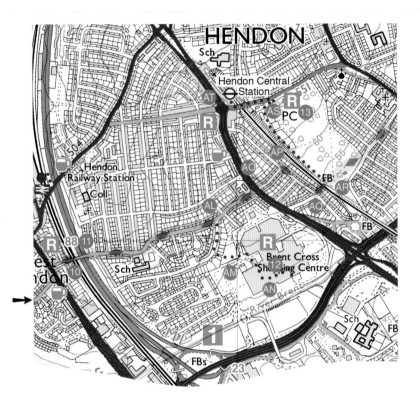

The Capital Ring follows Park Road across the main railway line **10** from St Pancras to the East Midlands and Yorkshire, opened in 1868 for the Midland Railway, which now also carries Thameslink trains. Welsh Harp Station, now demolished, lay to the right of the bridge. Then comes the M1 **11**, Britain's first motorway, opened in 1959, although this section is a southward extension opened in 1974. During World War II, this area reverberated with the sound of warplanes using Hendon Aerodrome, a mile to the north. This was one of Britain's first aviation centres, famed for its air displays between the wars. Though the airfield is now closed, parts of its grounds are occupied by the RAF Museum and the Hendon Police College.

Park Road rises and falls, snaking past Parkfield Primary School. At Sturgess Avenue **AL**, over to your right is the massive Brent Cross Shopping Centre **12**, with 120 shops under one roof, as well as a wide choice of eateries and toilets. *If this is irresistible, you can reach it by turning right at Sturgess Avenue, then in 150 yards, between house numbers 31 and 33, turn left along a footpath, keep ahead through a small park, go over a zebra crossing* **AM***, then bear left. You can finish the walk here, if you wish, as the centre has its own bus station* **AN** *(0.4 miles/0.7 km off route).*

The Capital Ring continues along Park Road as it bears left uphill to A41 Hendon Way **AO**, which you cross through a ramped subway to the left.

Hendon has a connection with David Garrick, the great 18th-century actor. At a time when being 'lord of the manor' was still a real status symbol, he bought the ancient manor of Hendon at auction. The land had previously belonged to the Herbert family, later the Earls of Pembroke and Marquises of Powys.

On the far side of the subway, turn right up the ramp, then turn left along Beaufort Gardens. At the end, cross and turn right along Cheyne Walk **AP**. Crowning the hill ahead is one of London's best-known open spaces, Hampstead Heath. In 200 yards, at the junction with Renters Avenue **AQ**, turn left along a tarmac path and climb 23

steps up and down to cross a footbridge over the Northern Line's Edgware branch. The bridge leads into Hendon Park **13**, where Walk 10 finishes **AR**. To your left, inside the park, lies one of the Millennium Woods planted in 2000 by Barnet schoolchildren. *Walk 11 continues ahead along the path with lampposts.*

> **Capital Ring link to Hendon Central Station** *(0.5 miles / 0.8 km). Turn left at the foot of the steps from the footbridge **AR** along a tarmac path beside the railway. Follow the path all the way to the top, past tennis courts, then turn right past the park's café and toilets towards the Holocaust Memorial Garden. Turn left out of the park, cross Queen's Road **AS** at the refuge, then turn left again to the traffic lights at Hendon Way, where you turn right to Hendon Central Station **AT** (cafés)*

The 'seaside creek' at Hendon Waterside.

11 Hendon Park to Highgate

Distance 5.3 miles (8.5 km). Excludes Capital Ring links of 0.4 miles (0.7 km) from Hendon Central Station and 0.1 miles (0.1 km) to Highgate Station.

Public transport The start of Walk 11 is in Hendon Park, just under half a mile from Hendon Central Station and buses. The route passes East Finchley Station. The finish is in Priory Gardens, 120 yards from Highgate Station. All stations on this walk are in Travelcard Zone 3, but Hendon Central is in both Zones 3 and 4.

Surface and terrain Most of the route is on paving, tarmac or bonded gravel, and generally fairly level. The central section of half a mile includes some uneven paths with short but fairly steep ascents and descents, and the last half-mile in Queen's Wood is on steep paths, which can be avoided by following nearby roads.

Refreshments Hendon Central, Temple Fortune, Hampstead Garden Suburb, East Finchley, Cherry Tree Wood, Highgate Wood, Queen's Wood and Highgate.

Toilets Lyttelton Playing Fields, Cherry Tree Wood and Highgate Wood.

Capital Ring link from Hendon Central Station. From the station exit A, turn left, then left again along Queen's Road, past some of the station bus stops. Go over the railway line, past Wykeham Road, then cross Queen's Road at the refuge. Turn left, then in 30 yards turn right into Hendon Park B. Bear half-right, with the Holocaust Memorial Gardens on your left, then turn right past the tennis courts, park café and toilets. Turn left on a tarmac path along the edge of the park to the footbridge C bringing walk 10 of the Capital Ring into the park, where you turn left.

Walk 11 of the Capital Ring starts in Hendon Park **1**, in the London Borough of Barnet. Keep ahead along the path with lampposts and continue along Shirehall Lane **D**. Pass Park View Gardens and Elms Avenue, then take the next right turn into Shirehall Close

E. At the end, turn left along Shirehall Park **F** and bear left with the road. In 40 yards turn right along a short link road, using the left-hand pavement, to reach A502 Brent Street **G**.

Cross Brent Street at the refuge and turn right. As you cross the River Brent, look left to see two pepperpot gazebos on either side of a weir. They survive from a time when the gardens on either side belonged to the Brent Bridge Hotel, demolished in 1974. During the 'Dance Band Days' of the 1920s and 30s, this was the venue of Pat O'Malley's Romany Band, one of the leading outfits of that period. Ahead lies the A406 North Circular Road **H**, built during the 1920s, which carries some 85,000 vehicles a day along its 25 miles. It has the dubious distinction of being the noisiest road in Britain and will make its presence felt for the next mile. **Turn left beside it for 150 yards, then after Brook Lodge turn left through a gate I into Brent Park 2 (see box on map below).** Not to be confused with the massive trading estate further west, this pretty little park is the first of several open spaces along this stretch of the Capital Ring, resulting from a policy of leaving such areas undeveloped in case of flooding. Ignoring the footbridge to your left (which carries the alternative route described on the map), keep ahead for 250 yards, walking among trees on a winding tarmac path, beside or close to the River Brent, with the North Circular Road to your right.

Parklands

Despite the proximity of the North Circular Road, the Capital Ring manages to find a pleasant route through adjacent parkland.

At the next path junction, turn sharp left around a pond. You continue between the river and the pond, known as The Decoy **3**, where ducks were lured for capture. At the end of the pond, the path swings right, then you turn left to leave the park through a gate into Bridge Lane **J**. Cross over and turn left for 50 yards, then turn right beside the river along a tarmac path called Brookside Walk. You shortly reach the point beside a playground **K** where Dollis Brook (from ahead) and Mutton Brook (from the right) merge to form the River Brent. Dollis Brook rises at Moat Mount, near Scratchwood Services on the M1; Mutton Brook rises near Highgate.

Please note: The noisy route beside the A406, described in blue above and marked blue on the map, can be avoided as follows, though not officially part of the Capital Ring. Just before the bus stop in Brent Street **G**, turn left along a footpath among bushes, which leads beside housing and across a footbridge directly into Brent Park **2**, where you turn left at a path junction **I**.

Edwardian children gardening behind one of the houses in Hampstead Garden Suburb.

For the next mile you join the Dollis Valley Greenwalk, which follows Dollis Brook from Moat Mount and Barnet, and then turns along Mutton Brook. Turn right along a tarmac path that leads beside Mutton Brook and through a tunnel under the North Circular Road. Keep ahead on a very narrow path, which rises and falls through a long, grassy open space, still with the brook on your right and the North Circular Road now away to your left. In places the surface is uneven and stony, and may be muddy. Eventually, you rise quite steeply to reach A598 Finchley Road at Henly's Corner *(buses, cafés up to your right)*.

Cross Finchley Road carefully at the traffic lights **L**. On the far side, look left, beyond the North Circular and a bus stop, for a distant view of a bronze sculpture that gives this junction its unofficial local name: 'The Naked Lady' **4**. Its proper name is *La Délivrance*, by Emile Guillaume, and it commemorates the alliance of British and French troops at the Battle of the Marne in 1914. Keep ahead down a steep tarmac path, then cross a footbridge over Mutton Brook and climb to the right of it, not quite reaching a road **M**. Bear left behind the houses, still close to the brook. At a path junction keep ahead, with Mutton Brook emerging from a culvert nearby, then turn right into Addison Way **N**. Turn left for 150 yards to reach a spur road linking Addison Way with the parallel A1 Falloden Way *(buses)*. Here the Dollis Valley Greenwalk splits off to the right towards its eventual target, Hampstead Heath, while the Capital Ring continues ahead, now beside the A1 Falloden Way. After crossing Mutton Brook **O**, turn right along a tarmac path into Northway Gardens **5**, and follow it round to the left, with the brook to your right. At a path intersection, keep ahead towards a black shelter, left of the brook, with tennis courts on the far bank. At the shelter, bear right then left, staying on the brook's left bank. After more tennis courts, fork left to

reach a road, Northway **P**, in Hampstead Garden Suburb beside Café Toulous, wittily named after the ladies' and gents' toilets from which it was converted *There are buses and another café in Market Place to your left.* This settlement was the brainchild of Henrietta Barnett, a leading philanthropist and social reformer. In 1906, she set up a trust to acquire land in the area, partly to extend Hampstead Heath, but mostly to develop an integrated community, where people from all backgrounds could live in pleasant surroundings. This brave social experiment only lasted for a decade or two before commercial pressures took over; the area has since become one of the most affluent parts of London.

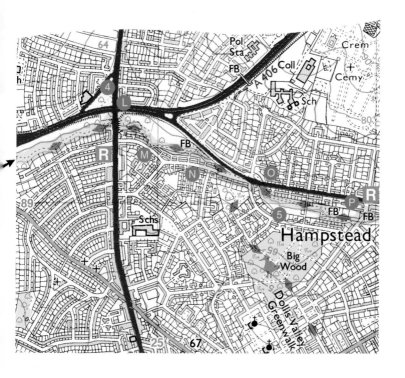

Cross Northway and keep ahead into the next part of Northway Gardens, with Mutton Brook still to your right. Cross Kingsley Way **Q** and turn right over the brook, then turn left past a barrier into Lyttelton Playing Fields **6**. You have now entered the territory of what used to be the Bishop of London's extensive hunting park, which was created in the 13th century and extended well to the east from here. At a fork, bear right, away from the brook. The route bends left to pass a children's playground, then left again near a pavilion *(toilets and seasonal kiosk)*. Turn right past tennis courts and a bowling green, then the path swings right and left to leave the park into a road called Norrice Lea **R**.

Queen's Wood near Highgate, once known Churchyard Bottom Wood, was renamed the late 19th century after Queen Victori

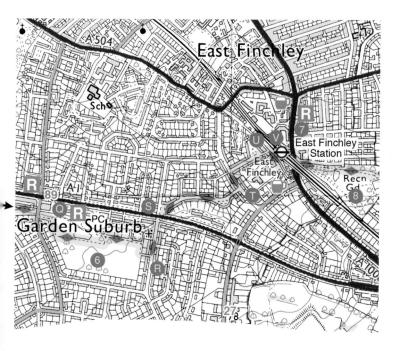

Turn left, passing Hampstead Garden Suburb Synagogue, to reach A1 Lyttelton Road **S** *(buses)*.

Cross at the lights, then turn right and immediately left into Vivian Way. Follow it round to the right, then in 250 yards you reach a little green, where the road swings left to reach Deansway **T**. Cross over and turn left, then in 80 yards turn right up Edmund's Walk. At the top, by another little green, keep ahead along a narrow path to a T-junction. Turn right along a broader path called The Causeway **U** to arrive at the back entrance of East Finchley Station **V**. You should be able to go through the station subway to the A1000 Great North Road. *If the subway is closed, continue along The Causeway to the Great North Road and turn left under the bridge past the While Lion pub and bus stops to reach*

the traffic lights. Look up above the station entrance to see *The Archer*, a bold statue firing an arrow along the railway line towards Highgate. Uphill, on the opposite side of the road, you can just see the sign of the venerable Phoenix Cinema **7**, opened in 1910 as the East Finchley Picturedrome. Cross over at the traffic lights. The Great North Road leads from London through Finchley to the north of England and eventually to Edinburgh, a distance of some 400 miles (640 km). From at least the 14th century, this was the main route to the north, replacing the Roman Ermine Street further east.

On the far side of the road, turn right. In 20 yards turn left at a low brick wall before the bridge, then bear right through a gate into a park called Cherry Tree Wood **8**. Unsurprisingly renamed from the original Dirthouse

Wood, it is a remnant of the ancient Forest of Middlesex and of the Bishop of London's hunting park. Keep ahead along a tarmac path past a playground. Leave the park, passing toilets and a seasonal refreshment kiosk, and proceed ahead along Fordington Road **W**, now in the London Borough of Haringey. At the junction with Woodside Avenue **X**, cross via a refuge and go up Lanchester Road opposite. In 50 yards turn left up a steep tarmac path between fences. At the top you cross the disused and overgrown track of the former branch line from Finsbury Park to Alexandra Palace, which later forms part of Walk 12 of the Capital Ring. Pass through Bridge Gate **Y** into Highgate Wood **9**, previously known as Gravel Pit Wood, another remnant of the Forest of Middlesex. It is one of the many parcels of open space that were acquired by the Corporation of London during the 19th century so that they could be maintained in perpetuity for Londoners' recreation, at a time when any open space within reach of the City was under pressure for housing development.

Keep ahead on the stony path to an intersection **Z**. On the left is a disused granite drinking fountain, erected in 1888, with separate troughs for horses and dogs. It bears a quotation from 'Inscription for a fountain on a heath', penned in 1802 by Samuel Taylor Coleridge. Turn right at the fountain along a tarmac track to the next junction **AA**. *Just a few yards ahead are the park café and toilets.* A plaque marks the spot where the

Capital Ring was formally launched on 21 September 2005. The Capital Ring goes left here, then keeps ahead to go past a lodge. Keep ahead at a crossing track then fork left to leave the woods through New Gate beside traffic lights. Cross B550 Muswell Hill Road **AB** and enter Queen's Wood **10**. The next section through Queen's Wood has very steep ascents and descents; an alternative route to avoid these is shown in the panel below.

> ### Alternative route to Highgate Station avoiding Queen's Wood
> *After crossing Muswell Hill Road **AB**, turn right up it for 400 yards to traffic lights at the corner of Wood Lane **AG**, just before the main Archway Road. Cross and turn left into Wood Lane, then immediately turn right down a steep tarmac path to Highgate Station **AF**. Alternatively, you can continue to the main road, where there are buses, and if you are continuing on to Walk 12 turn left down Archway Road to rejoin the Capital Ring at the junction with Shepherd's Hill (page 124, point **D**).*

Queen's Wood is a complete contrast to Highgate Wood: less visited, much hillier and an altogether wilder atmosphere, the result of careful planning by the London Borough of Haringey to maintain the natural balance. This used to be known as Churchyard Bottom Wood until the late 19th century, when it was acquired by Hornsey Council and renamed after Queen Victoria. Note the wood's own idiosyncratic signposts. Go down the path to the Woodkeeper's Lodge **11**. Built in 1898, the lodge is now the Queen's Wood Café, a showpiece of environmentally friendly urban living. Food from the lodge's organic garden is served in its café, open daily. Bear right down a tarmac path, then at the bottom, by a fence corner and signpost, take the right fork, passing a fallen tree. Climb a steep gravel path, which bears left and levels out at the top.

At the next path junction, fork right up to Queen's Wood Road **AC** and cross over to the next part of the

New Names

Unsurprisingly, Dirthouse, Gravel Pit and Churchyard Bottom Woods have been renamed. All is revealed here.

wood. The path rises over a crossing path, then bears left down steps to the foot of the hill, by a low brick wall. Turn right up a steep tarmac path to the road, Priory Gardens **AD**, and turn right. Walk 11 finishes in 250 yards, opposite a narrow footpath between house numbers 63 and 65 **AE**.

*To continue on Walk 12, turn left up this path. For Highgate Station **AF** (refreshment kiosk), continue ahead along Priory Gardens for 120 yards. For buses in Archway Road, go through the station ticket office and up the escalator.*

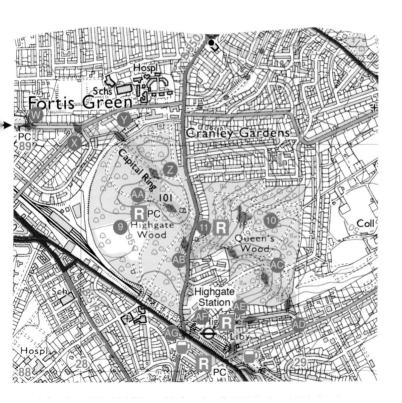

12 Highgate to Stoke Newington

Distance 5.4 miles (8.5 km). Excludes Capital Ring links of 0.1 miles (0.1 km) at each end.

Public transport The start of Walk 12 is 120 yards from Highgate Station. There are Capital Ring links with Crouch Hill, Finsbury Park and Manor House Stations. The finish is 100 yards from Stoke Newington Station. Highgate and Crouch Hill Stations are in Travelcard Zone 3, Finsbury Park is in Zone 2 but Manor House is in both Zones 2 and 3.

Surface and terrain The first 150 yards are on a very steep tarmac path, but this can be avoided. After that, the route is almost completely level. The Parkland Walk has a rolled-gravel track for nearly 2 miles but may be muddy in places. From Finsbury Park onwards the route is on tarmac or paving but the path beside the New River is mostly on grass or earth and may be muddy in places and has a short flight of steps – this can be avoided on an alternative route. There is an avoidable flight of seven steps at Abney Park Cemetery.

Refreshments Highgate, Crouch End, Stroud Green, Finsbury Park, Manor House, The Castle, Clissold Park and Stoke Newington.

Toilets Highgate, Finsbury Park, The Castle, Clissold Park and Abney Park Cemetery.

Capital Ring link from Highgate Station. From the ticket barriers, turn left out of the station A into Priory Gardens and keep ahead along the right-hand pavement for 120 yards to the footpath between house numbers 63 and 65. You join the Capital Ring here. Walk 11 comes up Priory Gardens in the opposite direction.

Walk 12 starts from Priory Gardens, in the London Borough of Haringey, by climbing the narrow, steep tarmac footpath between house numbers 63 and 65 **B** into Highgate Spinney. *This can be avoided by using the escalator from Highgate Station to Archway Road **C**, where turn left for 150 yards down to the junction at **D**, then keep ahead.*

Using the footpath from Priory Gardens, on reaching Shepherd's Hill beside Highgate Library, turn right to the junction

with Archway Road **D**. Ahead lies a red-brick building. Previously Highgate Methodist Church, it is now Jackson's Lane Community Centre **1**, with a theatre, café and toilets. Turn left at the lights and go down Archway Road for 50 yards to the next junction. From here, beside the Boogaloo pub, you can see the Archway **2**, after which this road is named. Archway Road is in effect a bypass for Highgate village, which lies up Southwood Lane, on your right. It was built to avoid the very steep Highgate Hill and was to have gone through a tunnel, but this collapsed during construction in 1812 to leave a huge chasm with no crossing point. A brick bridge provided the initial remedy, and this was replaced in 1900 by the graceful iron structure now known as the Archway.

Turn left down Holmesdale Road and follow it round to the right, then at the next bend turn left through a gate **E** into the Parkland Walk **3**. To your left is the end of a disused tunnel, once used by trains but now a bat roost and hibernaculum. The Capital Ring turns right, following for nearly 2 miles (3 km) the gradually descending former railway line, now a rolled-gravel track, which is much used by cyclists.

The Parkland Walk began life as the Edgware, Highgate & London Railway, opened in 1867 from Finsbury Park to Edgware, with branches added to High Barnet (1872) and Alexandra Palace (1873), but it was never very successful. During the 1930s, work started on electrifying the route as a branch of the Northern Line, but World War II got in the way and the plan was abandoned. The line closed to passenger traffic in 1954, and to other traffic in 1970, then the track was

Be prepared for the spriggan emerging from the brickwork soon after the abandoned Crouch End Station.

eventually acquired by the London Borough of Haringey. Despite a threat to build a motorway, in 1984 the Parkland Walk became London's longest linear park, and later a nature reserve, providing a haven for wildlife in a densely populated area.

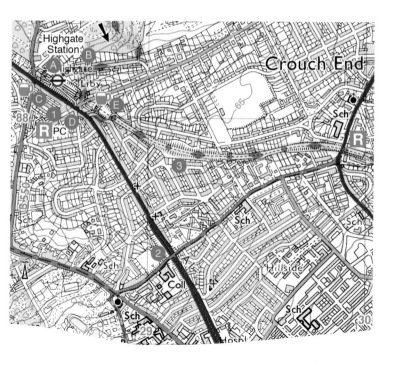

Highgate to Stoke Newington

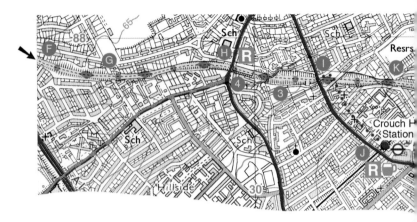

The first part of the Parkland Walk follows an embankment over Northwood Road **F** and Stanhope Road **G**. It continues through a cutting, passing under Crouch End Hill **H** *(buses and café accessible via a path up to the left)*. Immediately afterwards are the platforms of the abandoned Crouch End Station **4**. The Parkland Walk now passes under a footbridge, which marks the start of a short stretch of about 600 yards in the London Borough of Islington. With some trepidation, look up to your left to see, emerging from the brickwork, a 'spriggan' – a fearsome mythical creature from local folklore. Pass the Cape Adventure Playground, where there is access to Crouch Hill **I** *(buses)* via a tarmac path to your left.

The Parkland Walk

Once destined to be turned into a motorway, the Parkland Walk was saved by local activists working with Haringey and Islington Councils. It is now a 2-mile-long nature reserve.

The Parkland Walk continues in a cutting under Crouch Hill and Mountview Road, then runs beside Blythwood Road and passes a tree trail and an area of rare acid grassland. Back in Haringey borough you cross Mount Pleasant **K** then follow a series of embankments. To your left is a grass-covered reservoir, while to your right in the distance can be seen The Shard and high-rise blocks in East London. Crossing Stapleton Hall Road **L** *(buses and the Nicholas Nickleby pub)* in Stroud Green, you find yourself on the topmost of three levels of transport, with the road below and the Gospel Oak to Barking railway line beneath that. This was the site of Stroud Green Station, though there is virtually nothing left of it. The route

*Capital Ring link with Crouch Hill Station (0.3 miles / 0.4 km). Take the path up to Crouch Hill **I**, then turn right for 400 yards downhill, using the zebra crossing to continue on the opposite side to Crouch Hill Station **J** (Old Dairy pub and cafés nearby). If starting here, turn right uphill for 400 yards, using the zebra crossing to continue on the opposite side. At the top, just after the bridge, turn left down the paved path **I** and turn left again at the foot.*

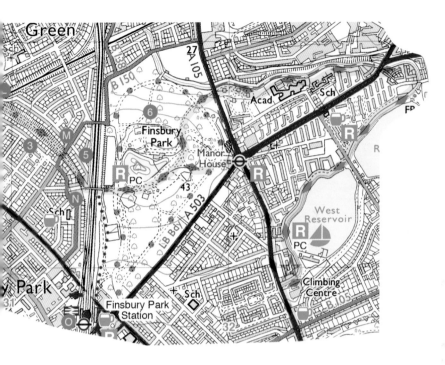

crosses Upper Tollington Park **M**. *A little white tower that appears to your right, with a wind vane, sits atop Stroud Green Primary School beside which lies the Faltering Fullback pub.* At the end of the Parkland Walk, bear left over a footbridge **N** into Finsbury Park. Below it runs the East Coast Main Line **5** from London to Scotland, which opened in 1850 for the Great Northern Railway and was incorporated into the London & North Eastern Railway system in 1923.

Finsbury Park **6**, one of the largest open spaces in North London, developed around the old Hornsey Wood. It opened in 1862 as a replacement for the pleasure grounds taken from the people of Finsbury, a more central part of London.

Capital Ring link with Finsbury Park Station *(0.4 miles / 0.6 km).*
*Immediately after the footbridge **N**, inside Finsbury Park, turn right beside a fence, parallel with the railway line. Follow this for 500 yards down to the foot of the hill, then at a path junction turn right, passing a cycle park, to Stroud Green Road, where go over the pedestrian crossing to Finsbury Park bus and train stations **O**. If starting here, from the main train station exit (Station Place) turn left through the bus station and go over the pedestrian crossing towards Rowans Leisure Centre on the far side of Stroud Green Road. Turn left, then shortly right by a high brick wall into Finsbury Park, passing the cycle park. Fork left, then shortly turn left to follow a footpath close to the park fence for 500 yards to the top, by the footbridge **N**, where turn right to join the Capital Ring.*

This contraption beside the New River is used to clear weed from a sluice.

Keep ahead across the park service road **P** and along a winding path with the park café and toilets over to your left. *The park's boating lake is a little to the left here.* Just past the red-brick Furtherfield Gallery, turn right through an area with flowerbeds. Keep ahead on a path, which veers to the left to reach a major path junction **Q** with a Capital Ring main sign beside a three-pronged pedestrian shelter.

---

*Alternative route to Clissold Park via Manor House Station. The route beside the New River mostly follows grass and earth paths, and has a short flight of steps. You can avoid them (and reach Manor House Station) by turning right at the path junction **Q**. Cross the park service road and pass through the ceremonial gateway. Manor House Station **R** can be reached by any of several staircases here. To continue to Clissold Park turn right across Seven Sisters Road, then left over Green Lanes. Turn right to follow Green Lanes for 700 yards to the gate by The Castle **V**, where you rejoin the main route. This alternative reduces the distance of Walk 12 by about three-quarters of a mile (1.4 km).*

The main route continues ahead with a sports arena to your left. At the next junction, keep ahead and shortly re-cross the service road to leave the park on to A105 Green Lanes **7**, where you enter the London Borough of Hackney. This busy North London artery originally consisted of several separate lanes that linked a series of village greens, hence the unusual plural form of the name. Cross over at the traffic lights, then turn left and in 20 yards turn right through gate **S** to join the New River Path, distinguishable by its bright green signposts.

The New River **8** is neither new nor a river. It is an unnavigable artificial watercourse, completed in 1613 to bring fresh water to London from springs near Ware in Hertfordshire. To achieve this, Sir Hugh Myddelton, the Welsh engineer, devised an ingenious 40-mile course that closely followed the contours of the land, dropping about 2 inches every mile, so that gravity draws the water along. Nowadays the water flows only as far as the Stoke Newington reservoirs. Until recently, there was no access to the grassy banks, but the New River Path now follows them where possible, courtesy of Thames Water, all the way to Hertfordshire.

The Capital Ring runs along the river's right bank for more than a mile, with one short break. To your right stretches Woodberry Down, Britain's largest council housing estate, comprising over 50 blocks of flats. At A503, Seven Sisters Road **T**, the route continues opposite, but as this road is usually very busy you should use the protected crossings to your left, then return along the far side.

Highgate to Stoke Newington

Continuing beside the river, in 250 yards cross a lane (Newnton Close) to come alongside Stoke Newington's East Reservoir **9**. A bonded gravel path winds beside The New River and the reservoir, around which a new nature reserve called Woodberry Wetlands has been created, with a café and toilets. Cross Lordship Road **U**, with a café and supermarket nearby. The path continues ahead, now beside the West Reservoir **10**, which has a sailing club. A footbridge leads to the Thames Water depot, where the building to the left has a café and toilets. Here stands another of the disguised pumping stations built by the water companies of yesteryear. This one, constructed in 1855 with turrets and battlements, is known as The Castle **11**.

Superfluous to requirements an[d] machinery, it is now a first-class [indoor] climbing centre, with a café and to[ilets for] public use, though they can only be [reached] up long flights of stairs. Turn right throu[gh] the depot to the gate **V**, then left along the main road – Green Lanes again. Keep ahead at traffic lights, then in 200 yards turn left through a gate **W** into Clissold Park **12**, named after the Rev. Augustus Clissold. A local parson, during the 19th century he courted his beloved, Eliza Crawshay, against the will of her father, who hated parsons and owned the mansion then known as Paradise House. They courted in secret, but were only able to marry after the demise of Mr Crawshay, and promptly renamed the mansion Clissold House.

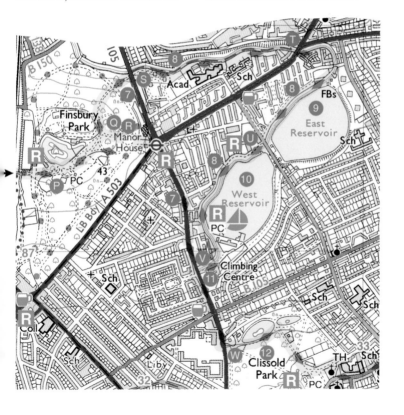

The magnificent spire of St Mary's Church in Stoke Newington soars 220 feet above Clissold Park. Its older sister church lies behind the trees on the left.

The two small lakes ahead were formed by damming Hackney Brook, and are named after the park's founders. Keep ahead along the right bank of the first, Beckmere **X**. Just before the second, Runtzmere, turn sharp right along an avenue of turkey-oak and horse-chestnut trees. At the far end, with the magnificent spire of St Mary's Church **14** soaring ahead, you pass a playground to reach Clissold House **13**. An extensive renovation of the house, which contains a café and toilets, was completed in 2011.

Turn left at the house, past the playground, and fork left, with the spire now to your right. The smaller Ancient Mother Church **15** appears on your right, after which you turn right through a gate **Y** and follow a fenced footpath through the graveyard. Turn left at Stoke Newington Church Street.

During the 17th and 18th centuries, the village of Stoke Newington became a refuge for dissenters and nonconformists excluded from the City of London. One of these was Daniel Defoe (1660–1731), writer, political activist and secret agent, who lived in Church Street and is of course most famous for *Robinson Crusoe* and *Moll Flanders*. His name lives on in the names of a street, a school and a pub. The two parish churches of Stoke Newington face each other across Church Street. The older and smaller of the two, built in 1563, is the old St Mary's, now called the Ancient Mother Church. The larger and more imposing one opposite, with its 220-foot spire, is the new St Mary's, designed by George Gilbert Scott and consecrated in 1858.

At just under 4 miles (6.4 km) from Charing Cross, this is as close as the Capital Ring gets to central London. Keep ahead along the left-hand pavement of Church Street, passing Stoke Newington Town Hall **16**, then Stoke Newington Library **17** and several pubs and cafés. Budding musicians may wish to window-shop at Bridgewood & Neitzert (number 146) – though only established in 1983, they have become one of the UK's leading dealers of stringed instruments.

Soon after the Daniel Defoe pub (a blue plaque opposite marks the site of his home), turn left through a small gate **Z** and climb seven steps into Abney Park Cemetery **18**. *The steps can be avoided by continuing ahead to the High Street* **AA***, then turning left for a few yards to the main gates of the cemetery.* Abney Park Cemetery is a cheerfully eerie place, whose 300,000 graves are framed by foliage amid an air of controlled abandonment. It is owned by the London Borough of Hackney, which has set up a trust to prevent further decay without spoiling

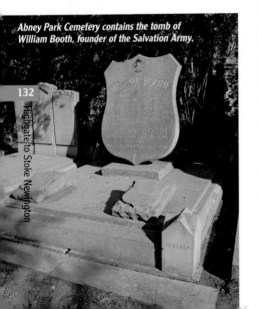

Abney Park Cemetery contains the tomb of William Booth, founder of the Salvation Army.

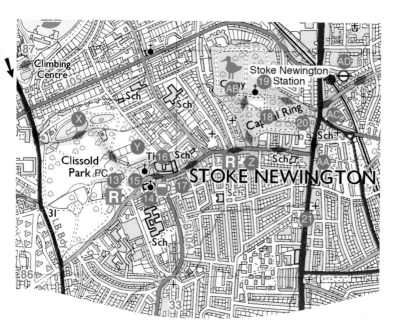

the habitats that have made this an official nature reserve. The cemetery was laid out in 1840 but never consecrated, enabling the many religious dissenters that lived in this area to be buried here.

Inside the cemetery, keep ahead along a narrow path between graves, then at the main path turn left. Almost opposite is the tomb of William Booth (1829–1912), founder of the Salvation Army, and his wife, Catherine, while next to it are buried several other early Salvation Army luminaries. Turn left along the main path to an intersection **AB**, where you turn right to pass the derelict chapel **19** of 1840, with its towering steeple, at the centre of the cemetery. A short distance to the right is an impressive war memorial, one of thousands around the world maintained by the Commonwealth War

Graves Commission, which was established in 1917. Beyond that the grave of and memorial to Isaac Watts (1674–1748), the nonconformist preacher and hymn-writer. Keep ahead towards the main gate into Stoke Newington High Street. The cemetery's visitor centre is located in the lodge **20** on your right, where Capital Ring walkers may use the toilets.

Pass through the main gate, then turn left along A10 Stamford Hill. Cross at the lights to the junction with Cazenove Road **AC**, where Walk 12 ends. The dead-straight A10, or Great Cambridge Road, follows the line of Ermine Street **21**, the Roman road from London through Lincoln to York. *To continue to Walk 13, keep ahead along Cazenove Road. Stoke Newington Station **AD** is 150 yards to the left up Stamford Hill, with bus stops nearby.*

13 Stoke Newington to Hackney Wick

Distance 3.7 miles (6.0 km). Excludes Capital Ring links of 0.1 miles (0.1 km) from Stoke Newington Station and 0.3 miles (0.5 km) to Hackney Wick Station.

Public transport The start of Walk 13 is 150 yards from Stoke Newington Station and close to bus stops. There is a Capital Ring link with Clapton Station. It finishes 500 yards from Hackney Wick Station and bus stops. Stoke Newington and Hackney Wick Stations are in Travelcard Zone 2 but Clapton Station is in both Zones 2 and 3.

Surface and terrain The route is almost entirely level, but in Springfield Park there is a short and fairly steep descent including a flight of steps (avoidable via a diversion). There are some very short but quite steep ascents and descents on the Lee Navigation towpath. Most of the route is on tarmac or paving, but much of the Lee Navigation towpath has an uneven surface and may be muddy in places.

Refreshments Stoke Newington, Springfield Park, Lea Bridge Road and Hackney Wick.

Toilets Springfield Park.

---

*Capital Ring link from Stoke Newington Station and buses. From the station exit **A**, turn left along Stamford Hill for 150 yards past some of the station bus stops to the junction with Cazenove Road **B**. You join the Capital Ring by turning left here.*

Walk 13 starts at the junction of Stamford Hill and Cazenove Road **B** in the London Borough of Hackney. Keep ahead along Cazenove Road, which is lined with magnificent centenarian plane trees, planted soon after 1900. In 300 yards you cross Alkham Road, then pass a green-domed building **1** on your right, actually a mosque that has been rather cleverly converted from several Victorian terrace houses. It is properly called Stamford Hill Masjid-e-Quba, named after the first mosque built by the Prophet Mohammed.

Take the next left, Kyverdale Road **C**, cross over and in 80 yards cross then turn right along Filey Avenue **D**, following it all the way to the main road, past Jubilee Primary School **E**. At A107 Clapton Common **F**, turn left and go over the zebra crossing, then turn right and immediately left along Springfield. In 100 yards keep ahead through the gate **G** into Springfield Park **2**.

Bear left past the lake, with the 19th-century Springfield House **3** on your left, *which has a café and toilets – note the poem on a poster on the lobby wall, 'Two giants of Springfield Park' by Sarah Couch (see below).* Pass between some bollards, turn right, then bear left downhill on a tarmac path. Ahead of you now is a good view across the Lea Valley towards Walthamstow. At a path junction, you pass the 'two giants' **4** (see above) – two tall beech trees. Continue ahead, descending more steeply, down six steps, along a path that bears right past tennis courts. *To avoid the steps, you can turn right at the 'two giants' and follow paths down the right-hand side of the park, though this is still steep.* At the next junction, leave the park through a gate **H**, then turn left past a barrier along a fenced tarmac path (Spring Lane) beside the Lee Navigation **5**. For centuries, the Lea formed the boundary between Essex and Middlesex, before the existence of Greater London, and now performs the same task between the London Boroughs of Hackney and Waltham Forest. For just as long, its spelling has caused many an argument. An early form was Ley, but Acts of Parliament insist on Lee, and Lea is how it appears

These beech trees are known as the 'two giants' of Springfield Park.

on many maps. An informal compromise has been reached whereby creations, such as the navigation and the regional park, are Lee, while natural manifestations, such as the river itself and the valley, are Lea. The river flows from the Chiltern Hills near Luton to the Thames at Bow Creek, and has provided

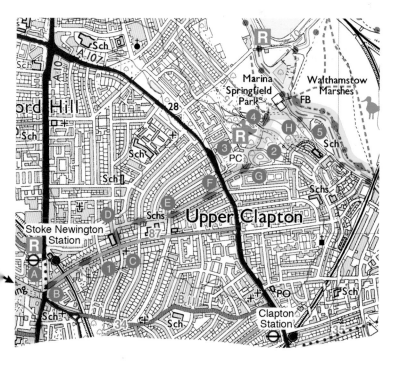

major route of communication since prehistoric times. The Lea Valley Walk follows the river for 50 miles (80 km) from near Luton to Bow Locks, and the Capital Ring joins it for the next 3 miles (5 km) – watch out for cyclists.

In 80 yards turn sharp right up a short but steep ramp to cross Horseshoe Bridge **I**, another typical canal crossover bridge, entering the London Borough of Waltham Forest. This stretch of the route is half green, that is, generally green on one side and built up on the other, with residential or commercial buildings. The skyline is sometimes dominated by power cables and pylons, but there is enough interest elsewhere to take your mind off them. To your left is Springfield Marina **6**, full of colourful narrowboats, which occupies the Coppermill Stream, a branch of the Lea. On the far side of the bridge, turn right, going steeply down, and keep ahead along a sand and gravel track parallel to the towpath, with some picnic tables nearby. A broad ditch separates you from Walthamstow Marsh Nature Reserve **7**, one of the few remaining areas of natural wetland in Greater London, where the dominant vegetation is sedge and reeds.

The view ahead is dominated by a viaduct through Clapton Junction **8**, which carries commuter trains and the Stansted Airport express service. It was in these arches that the aviator A. V. Roe constructed his early aeroplanes at the beginning of the 20th century. They were tested with flights across the marshes, which provided a mercifully soft surface for the many crash landings. Just before the railway bridge, the little Anchor & Hope pub **9** on the opposite bank cannot be reached – the

The Anchor & Hope pub lies tantalisingly out of reach on the far bank of the Lee Navigation.

High Hill Ferry that operated here ceased in the 1950s. The red-brick building nearby was once The Beehive pub. Beyond the bridge, away to the left soars the spire of St Saviours, the parish church of Walthamstow. The track rises a little to reveal a huge bubble ahead: it is the Lea Valley Ice Centre **10**, attracting skaters all year round. As you approach it, the river starts to bend right, then at a fingerpost you turn right across a long footbridge **J**, returning to Hackney borough.

Capital Ring link with Clapton Station *(0.4 miles / 0.7 km). As the river swings left, at North Millfields Park **K**, turn half-right into the park. Follow its right-hand side, turn left at the end, then turn right up Gunton Road to Upper Clapton Road, where you turn right to Clapton Station **L**. If starting here, turn left out of the station exit. In 30 yards turn left again down Gunton Road. Keep ahead along the left-hand side of North Millfields Park **K** to the Lee Navigation, where you turn right along the towpath.*

Continuing beside the Lee Navigation, you come to Lea Bridge **M**, carrying the very busy Lea Bridge Road *(buses)*. Pass under the bridge, then, with the terrace of the Princess of Wales pub on your right, the river and navigation separate for a while: the Old River Lea flows off to the left, while the Lee Navigation continues ahead. Soon afterwards, you cross Curtain Gate Bridge **N** and stay on the east bank for the rest of Walk 13. Behind a long brick wall lie the former Middlesex Filter Beds **11**, now a nature reserve. *It is worth going inside the gate and immediately turning left through a second gate to see the 'Ackney 'Enge – Hackney's version of Stonehenge – formed from the blocks that provided a base for a pumping engine.* The filter beds occupy the north end of Hackney Marsh **12**, on an island formed by the river and navigation. It is now occupied mostly by a vast sea of football pitches. When trees are bare, you can see a large building beyond, which is New Spitalfields Market, moved here from central London in 1991.

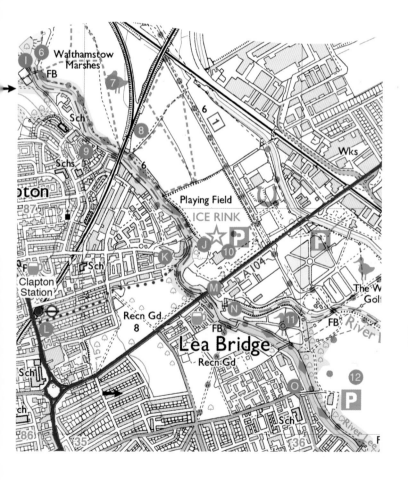

Ahead in the distance, the tops of the tallest buildings at Canary Wharf can be seen. Soon after a right-hand bend, you reach Cow Bridge **O**, painted in a rather bilious shade of lime green. The ornate gables peeping above houses belong to Mandeville Primary School, opened in 1902. Left- and right-hand bends lead under Daubeney Road footbridge to Marshgate Bridge **P**, carrying B112 Homerton Road *(buses)*. Immediately before the bridge, on the far bank, an apartment complex called Matchmakers Wharf **13** stands on the site of the former Lesney works, famed for its production of the highly collectable Matchbox toys, which are now made in Shanghai.

Continue along the towpath under the bridge. To your left now is Wick Woodland, while ahead looms the bridge of the A102M motorway, which has taken most of the traffic away from the old Eastway Bridge **Q** beyond. You have now reached the Queen Elizabeth Olympic Park **14**, stretching away to your left. It occupies what was the main centre for the London Olympic and Paralympic Games in 2012 (henceforth called 'the Games' in this

book), and has been redeveloped by the London Legacy Development Corporation to provide world-class sporting venues, attractive parklands, residential neighbourhoods and opportunities for business and employment. As well as celebrating the Games, the park was named to commemorate the Queen's Diamond Jubilee.

Ahead rises one of its main installations, the gigantic, convoluted steel structure called the ArcelorMittal Orbit, which you will pass in Section 14. The vast aluminium-clad building on your left, formerly the Press and Broadcast Centre for the Games, is now called Here East, a home for innovative individuals and companies seeking to develop new products and technology. To the right rise the twin windvane-topped towers of Gainsborough Primary School. You come to a new footbridge **R**, which now provides access to a more direct link with Hackney Wick Station (see text on map) than the official link described in the box. The dark, square building just past the footbridge is the Copper Box Arena, then a rust-coloured

At the north end of Hackney Marsh lies the 'Ackney 'Enge — all that remains of a pumping station in the former Middlesex Filter Beds

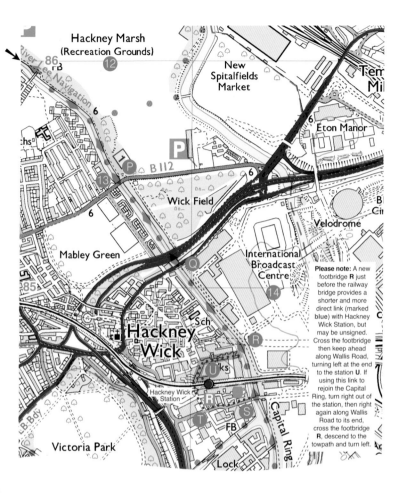

Please note: A new footbridge **R** just before the railway bridge provides a shorter and more direct link (marked **blue**) with Hackney Wick Station, but may be unsigned. Cross the footbridge then keep ahead along Wallis Road, turning left at the end to the station **U**. If using this link to rejoin the Capital Ring, turn right out of the station, then right again along Wallis Road to its end, cross the footbridge **R**, descend to the towpath and turn left.

tower is part of the Kings Yard Energy Centre. Finally, you pass under a railway bridge carrying the London Overground to reach Carpenters Road Bridge **S**, where Walk 13 ends, just across the boundary with the London Borough of Tower Hamlets. The white building opposite is actually called The White Building! It is a bar and restaurant which brews its own ales. Several other eateries have recently opened in this up-and-coming area. *Walk 14 continues along the towpath.*

Capital Ring link to Hackney Wick Station *(0.3 miles / 0.5 km). Go under the bridge S and turn sharp left up a steep, cobbled ramp to A115 Carpenters Road. Turn left across the bridge, where the road becomes White Post Lane. Keep to the left-hand pavement, continuing around the bend past The Griddlers café for 100 yards to a zebra crossing T. Turn right here along Hepscott Road and keep ahead past bus stops towards the bridge to find the entrances to Hackney Wick Station U on your right.*

The Greenway, seen here near Plaistow, was laid out on top of sewage pipes running from Hackney to Beckton (Walk 14).

4.9 miles (7.9 km). Excludes Capital Ring links of 0.3 miles (0.5 km) from Hackney Wick Station and 0.2 miles (0.3 km) to Royal Albert Station.

Public transport The start of Walk 14 is 500 yards from Hackney Wick Station and buses. The route passes Pudding Mill Lane Station and there is a link to West Ham Station. The finish in Beckton District Park is on a bus route and 350 yards from Royal Albert Station (Docklands Light Railway). All stations on this walk are in Travelcard Zone 3, except Hackney Wick in Zone 2, but Pudding Mill Lane, West Ham and Abbey Road are in both Zones 2 and 3

Surface and terrain Almost the entire route is on a hard surface, consisting of paving, tarmac or bonded gravel. The only exception is the first half-mile on a rough and narrow towpath, which may be wet and muddy at times. Nearly all the walk is level, but there are some short and fairly steep slopes. The Greenway is a permissive path, which is closed at night.

Refreshments Hackney Wick, Pudding Mill Lane, Plaistow.

Toilets Pudding Mill Lane, Plaistow and Beckton District Park.

Capital Ring link from Hackney Wick Station

*(0.3 miles / 0.5 km). From the station exits **A**, turn left and cross White Post Lane, then keep ahead along Hepscott Road, past the station bus stops, to A115 Rothbury Road **B**. Go over the zebra crossing and turn left. Keep ahead past The Griddlers café, now in White Post Lane again, and rise to the canal bridge. Ignore the towpath to the right before the bridge – this leads on to the Hertford Union Canal. Cross the bridge **C**, turn right through a railing and descend the steep cobbled ramp. You join the Capital Ring here. Walk 13 of the Capital Ring comes in from behind, under the bridge.*

Walk 14 starts at Carpenters Road Bridge **C** in the London Borough of Tower Hamlets. Keep ahead along the east (left) bank of the Lee Navigation, with the main Olympic stadium on your left. Opposite is the entrance to the Hertford Union Canal **1**, also known as Duckett's Cut after its promoter, Sir George Duckett, who got the canal through to completion in 1830. You can see the first of three locks that take it up past Victoria Park and on to the Regent's Canal at Bow Wharf. A new footbridge leads to an area known as Fish Island **2**, where some streets have fishy names. It was once notorious for foul-smelling industries, whose effluents polluted the river and canal, but they have closed down and a regeneration scheme is turning the district into a burgeoning business and residential area. Steps beside the footbridge provide access to the stadium.

The towpath rises at several points with rails leading off to the left – the remnants of crane tracks used for loading barges in the days when goods were largely transported on water. As you pass the stadium, on the opposite bank lies the factory of H. Forman & Son, appropriately painted salmon pink as they claim to be the world's oldest producer of smoked Scottish salmon. *It houses a restaurant and art gallery, which can be reached by crossing the twin Old Ford Locks **3**, a little further ahead.* The building on the left beside the locks, on the site of the lockkeeper's cottage, housed the studios of television production company Planet 24 and was the location for Channel 4's *Big Breakfast* until its demise in 2002. It is now a private house. Continue over a footbridge, where the Old River Lea rejoins the Navigation, and turn right to enter the London Borough of Newham for the rest of Walk 14. Turn right down the ramp. The Roman

road from London to Colchester, in use until the early 12th century, crossed the Lea hereabouts, hence the name Old Ford. It is believed to have been closed after Queen Maud, wife of Henry I, was unceremoniously, and presumably accidentally, ducked into the river. She ordered a new road to be built further south, now Stratford High Street.

A waterbus sign marks the point where some visitors to the Games were landed, but sadly this was discontinued afterwards. In a few more yards you pass under a bridge **D** to reach Greenway Turn, where you part company with the Lea Valley Walk. Immediately after the bridge, turn left up a tarmac ramp **E** to join a long embankment known as The Greenway **4**. The Greenway is a most imaginative use of sewage pipes: a level trackway of bonded gravel for walkers and

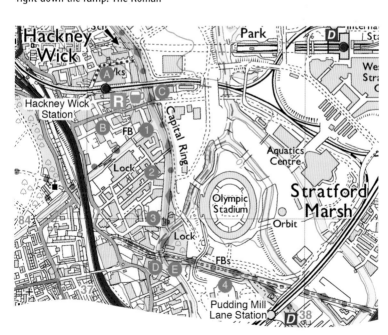

cyclists laid on top of the Northern Outfall Sewage Embankment – the acronym, NOSE, may have been deliberately chosen by an engineer with a sense of humour. The embankment runs for nearly 6 miles (9.6 km) from Hackney to Beckton, where the sewage is treated before discharge into the Thames. It is part of the extensive sewerage system designed for London in the 1860s by Sir Joseph Bazalgette, most of which still functions today. With four 9-inch pipes, the Northern Outfall is thought to contain the biggest sewage flow in Britain at over 100 million gallons a day. For the next
3 miles (5 km), the Capital Ring follows this engineering marvel, much of which was widened and refurbished for the purpose of bringing visitors to the Games. The Jubilee Greenway, previously encountered between Woolwich and Charlton, comes in from the left here and shares the Capital Ring's route all the way back to Woolwich, so you will once more see its distinctive waymark plaques set into the ground.

Turn right along the embankment. You now have a grandstand view of the Olympic Park, which covers 500 acres and stretches northwards from here for over a mile. Immediately on your left is the main Olympic Stadium **5**, which had 80,000 seats during the Games but has been downsized to become the new home of West Ham United Football Club. The area to your right was the athletes' warm-up area during the Games while the tall buildings of Canary Wharf rise in the distance. Next to the stadium is the extraordinary

ArcelorMittal Orbit **6**, designed by Sir Anish Kapoor and Cecil Balmond as an iconic centrepiece for the main Games venues and now providing spectacular views of the whole area from its upper decks, accessible by two lifts or a spiral staircase. Beyond the ArcelorMittal Orbit is the curved roof of the Games' Aquatic Centre, now a public swimming pool. These venues were due to re-open to the public in spring 2014. The unmissable melon-yellow building ahead is View Tube **7**, a community venue built from recycled shipping containers, with a café, toilets, viewing platforms, a wildlife garden and a multitude of interpretation boards.

The construction of Crossrail, linking Reading with Shenfield through Central London, currently blocks your progress, but it should soon be possible to continue ahead. For the present you must divert along roads. Just before View Tube, bear right down a ramp **F** then keep ahead along Marshgate Lane, under bridges **8** carrying the Docklands Light Railway and the main line from Liverpool Street to East Anglia, which opened in 1839 for the Eastern Counties Railway and later absorbed into the Great Eastern Railway. You pass Pudding Mill Lane Station **9** and swing right then left, crossing the City Mill River **10** to reach A11 Stratford High Street **G** *(buses)*. The river is the first of several channels that you cross in this area, collectively known as the Bow Back Rivers, that have been cut by the River Lea through this once marshy area. The Capital Ring encounters three of them.

Turn left along the High Street, then cross the Waterworks River **11**. Opposite is the latticed Strand East Tower, a remarkable structure in Dane's Yard **H**, part of an extensive residential and commercial development by Ikea.

Ahead of you now is Stratford town centre **12**, which has become one of the most vibrant parts of east London, benefiting from the legacy of the Games, with towering new offices and apartments and, half a mile away, the so-called 'mega-mall' of Westfield. Immediately opposite

Olympic Legacy

The legacy arrangements for the 2012 Olympic and Paralympic Games has ensured that this formerly run-down part of London is becoming 'top drawer'.

though, cowering in front of a skyscraper, is a comparatively tiny black-and-white building with a striking mural. Cross at the second set of traffic lights **I** then keep ahead to rejoin the Greenway. The left-hand side is now occupied by industry and warehousing, so looking to your right is a better bet. After passing Abbey Lane Recreation Ground **13**, you glimpse Canary Wharf again. On the bridge **14** over Abbey Lane, you re-cross the Meridian Line, marked by an iron sundial set in the ground.

Please note: Part of The Greenway is closed during construction of Crossrail, expected to be completed in 2017. Meanwhile the Capital Ring will follow a temporary route, approximately as shown, and as described in the text, but its exact line may change during the period of construction.

Appearing now through the trees is the eccentric old yellow-brick Abbey Mills Pumping Station **15**, looking like an oriental palace. The Grade II listed Victorian building, opened in 1868, was another part of Sir Joseph Bazalgette's immense scheme for ridding London of its sewage. With its cupola and gilded spire, and an interior like a Byzantine church, it suffered the soubriquet 'The Temple of Sewage' during its working life. Beyond it you can see the shimmering roof of the award-winning new pumping station **16**, opened in 1997. Just past the old pumping station, to your right, is a curious orange-and-yellow-painted metal object, shaped like a giant ammonite shellfish. Once part of the pumping station's machinery, it now provides an eyecatching piece of 'industrial sculpture'. The pump lies beside the

last and widest of the Bow Back Rivers, Channelsea **17**. Looking right as you cross, it splits into two, with Abbey Creek flowing to the right and Channelsea Creek to the left. These rivers are tidal and at low tide you may see wading birds feeding on the mud flats. The area to your left after the river was the site of Stratford Langthorne Abbey, from which this area takes its name. You cross Canning Road at surface level. *A workday café (open Mondays-Fridays) lies in the yard down to the right. Abbey Road Station on the Docklands Light Railway can be easily reached in 270 yards by turning left along Canning Road then right along Abbey Road, although this is not an official Capital Ring link.* Then a high-sided concrete bridge takes you over the Jubilee Line **19** and continues over Manor Road **J**. The link with West Ham

The Lee Navigation at Old Ford Lock, with the River Lea joining from the right.

Hackney Wick to Beckton Dist. Park

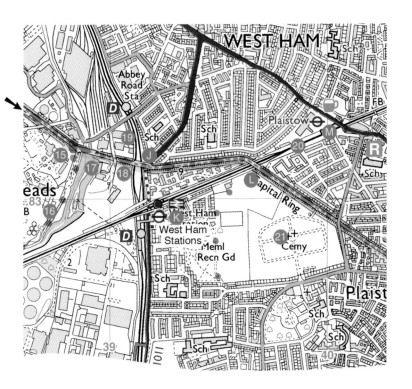

Station starts here (see next page), marked by the broad staircase that was installed for the hordes heading for the Games.

Ranelagh Primary School rises to the left behind houses, then The Greenway swings to the right, crossing the District Line and the London to Southend Railway **20**. *Just beyond this is an access point* **L** *signed Plaistow Station* **M**, *which is visible to your left – this is not a Capital Ring link, but you can reach it fairly easily in 500 yards by keeping close to the railway line.* You pass Memorial Park to your right, (look back for a fine view of The Shard and other well-known buildings in central London) then the East London Cemetery **21**. Among those buried here is the World War I German spy Carl Hans Lody, one of the last people to be executed at the Tower of London in 1914.

Capital Ring link to West Ham Station (0.1 miles / 0.2 km).
Immediately after crossing Manor Road **J**, *take the steps down to the right (or use the ramp a few yards further on), then turn left along Manor Road for 150 yards, crossing Alan Hocken Way, to West Ham Station* **K** *(café). If starting here, from the exit turn right and right again along Manor Road for 150 yards, crossing Alan Hocken Way. Just before the bridge, turn right up steps (or use the ramp) then turn right at the top along The Greenway.*

The old Abbey Mills Pumping Stati*
operating from 1868 to 1997, w*
known as 'The Temple of Sewag*

The Greenway comes to Upper Road **N**, the first of four busy roads in Plaistow *(all with buses)* which you cross in quick succession at surface level, via traffic lights. Next comes Balaam Street **O**. At Barking Road **P** is the grey-stone St Andrew's Church **22**, built in 1870, with its similar adjacent vicarage. After lying derelict for many years, it was restored in 1985 and is now the Universal Church of the Kingdom of God. Prince Regent Lane **Q**

soon follows. *There are cafés and buses to the left in Plaistow 23, along either of these last two roads.* The unusual name Plaistow (pronounced 'Plahstow') is thought to come from a Norman knight, Sir Hugh de Plaiz, plus 'stow', an Old English word meaning a place for meetings or sport. Beyond Prince Regent Lane, Newham University Hospital **24** spreads for several hundred yards along the right-hand side. Twelve large concrete balls mark

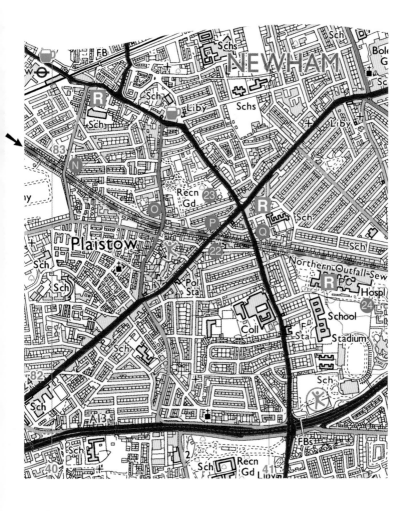

Boundary Lane **R**. Beyond that, with Brampton Manor Academy **25** on your right, you can see ahead the huge Barking Creek Flood Barrier, nearly 3 miles (5 km) away. Completed in 1982, it towers 193 feet (58 metres) above the mouth of the River Roding at its confluence with the Thames.

Soon after the end of the school playground, between two fences, you take your leave of The Greenway by turning right down steps or ramp **S**. Keep ahead along Stokes Road, then turn left along the misleadingly named Roman Road **T**, which is not Roman at all – it commemorates the discovery of Roman burials nearby in 1863, during gravel extraction for the NOSE. In 50 yards turn right into Noel Road **U** to reach A13 Newham Way **V**, which you cross on a footbridge with steps and ramps. Look left to see 'Beckton Alps': the giant slagheap of a former gasworks, grassed over and used for some years as a dry ski slope. On the far side, continue in the same direction past a blue fence along a street called Viking Gardens. To reach this you cross Jack Dash Way, named after the dockers' union leader who frequently hit the headlines in the 1950s and 1960s.

At the end of the street, continue ahead through a gate **W** into Beckton District Park **26**. On top of an apartment building to the left, note the wind vane depicting a ship and crane, another reminder of the dockworking background of this area (may not be visible in summer foliage).

The remainder of Walk 14 winds through this very pleasant park, bending first right then left along the main path. Ignore side turnings, but note that the right-hand side is a cycle track. The winding path is part of a tree trail, with marker plates describing the wide variety of unusual trees from all over the world. On reaching the first of several trim-trail fixtures, it is worth making a short diversion to the right to see the pretty lake **27** and its waterbirds. *The building at the far end has toilets.*

Cross Tollgate Road **X** at the refuge and continue on the main path through the park past houses. The path winds through meadows which are being managed to encourage wild flowers. Keep ahead past the Will Thorne Pavilion **28** and a playground, with Stansfeld Road to your right – *you can turn right here for Newham City Farm nearby (toilets).* Walk 14 ends at the next path junction **Y**. *To continue on to Walk 15, turn left here.*

Capital Ring link to Royal Albert DLR Station *(0.2 miles / 0.3 km). Turn right at the path junction **Y** and cross Stansfeld Road at the zebra crossing. Turn left for 150 yards to a roundabout at the junction with A1020 Royal Albert Way **Z**, passing the Jake Russell Walk bus stops. Bear right to cross the dual carriageway at the lights, then keep ahead along the fenced tarmac path to Royal Albert Station **AA** on the Docklands Light Railway.*

Hackney Wick to Beckton Dist. Park

15 Beckton District Park to Woolwich

Distance 3.5 miles (5.6 km). Excludes Capital Ring links 0.2 miles (0.3 km) from Royal Albert Station and 0.6 miles (0.9 km) to Woolwich Arsenal Station.

Public transport The start of Walk 15 is on a bus route and 350 yards from Royal Albert Station. The route passes Cyprus and Gallions Reach Stations, and there is a Capital Ring link with King George V Station. The finish is 100 yards from several bus routes and the Woolwich Free Ferry, and three-quarters of a mile from Woolwich Arsenal Station. All stations on this walk are in Travelcard Zone 3, except Woolwich Arsenal in Zone 4.

Surface and terrain Almost the entire walk is on a hard surface of paving or tarmac. It is entirely level apart from some very short slopes. Towards the end, the main route goes beside the River Thames, where there are several short flights of steps, lock gates and a short muddy path to negotiate in a somewhat desolate area. This can be avoided on an alternative route. There is the small matter of the Woolwich Foot Tunnel, which has over 100 steps on each side, though there are also lifts.

Refreshments UEL Campus, Galleons Point, North Woolwich and Woolwich.

Toilets UEL Campus, Beckton Community Centre and Woolwich.

---

*Capital Ring link from Royal Albert DLR Station (0.2 miles / 0.3 km). At the foot of the steps **A** from the platforms, turn back under the tracks (from the lifts keep ahead). Go through a gap in a fence and along a tarmac path to A1020 Royal Albert Way **B**. Keep ahead at the traffic lights over the dual carriageway, then turn right and bear left into Stansfeld Road, passing the Jake Russell Walk bus stops. Go over the zebra crossing to the path junction **C** in Beckton District Park.*

Walk 15 of the Capital Ring starts in Beckton District Park **1** at the path junction beside Stansfeld Road **C**, south of the Will Thorne Pavilion, where you are in the London Borough of Newham. The route continues through the park along a path beside a fenced trotting track, on the route of the former Beckton Railway. On the far side **D**,

turn right between trees, keeping close to houses on your left, then bear left to a path junction **E**. *Beckton Park DLR Station **F** is just 150 yards along a path to the right here, though this is not a Capital Ring link.* The Capital Ring continues ahead between the houses. At Harper Road/Parry Avenue, keep ahead along the right-hand side of the road (Savage Gardens), beside New Beckton Park **2**. In 200 yards, opposite Oakes Close **G**, turn right along a path across the park, beside the fence of the Stroud Pavilion.

Arriving at houses **H**, turn left along a footpath beside them, go through a barrier and past a playground. At Renfrew Rain Garden **I** keep ahead through another barrier beside a school to reach East Ham Manor Way **J**, opposite Beckton Community Centre, whose toilets can be used by

Capital Ring walkers. Turn right to pass a mini-roundabout then turn left across Strait Road **K** and keep ahead to a main sign. The Cyprus estate **3**, constructed in 1881, took its name from the British capture of the island a few years earlier.

Turn right across a footbridge, in between Cyprus DLR Station **L** below and Royal Albert Way above, into the Docklands Campus of the University of East London **4**. Keep ahead to the side of Royal Albert Dock **M**. There are cafés and toilets in the buildings on either side. When the site opened in 1999, it was the first new university campus built in London for over 50 years. Appropriately, it specialises in technology and multimedia, since the buildings were designed to maximise energy efficiency and were built on recycled soil. The University was formed in 1992 from the former North East London Polytechnic, and has another campus at Stratford. Student apartments with butterfly-wing roofs overlook the Royal Albert Dock **5**, over a mile long, which opened in 1880 and linked with two others to form the Royal Docks, in their day the largest in the world. Closed to commercial shipping in 1982, they continue in use as massive watersports facilities – Royal Albert has an Olympic-standard rowing course and stages regular regattas. On its far side is the runway of London City Airport **6**, opened in 1987 and fast expanding.

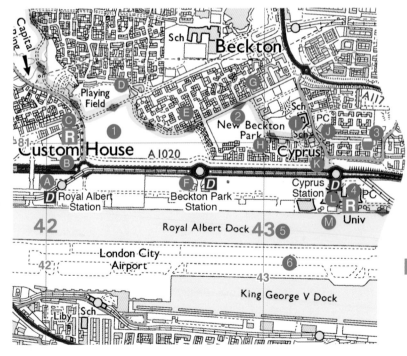

The student apartments of the University of East London's Docklands Campus overlook the Royal Albert Dock, now an Olympic standard rowing course.

Small craft can use Gallions Entrance Lock to access the marina inside it.

Turn left along the dockside promenade and follow it to the end. Approaching the end you pass Aqua East **7**, home of the UEL Student Union. Beyond this is the Sir Steve Redgrave Bridge **8**, opened in 1999 and replacing the original swing bridge. It was named in honour of the great rowing champion, born in 1962, who won gold medals at five successive Olympic Games and has close ties with Newham borough. The signed route now goes left to cross Gallions Roundabout **N**. However, a better but as yet unsigned alternative (marked blue on the map) can now be followed by continuing ahead under the bridge and turning left into the Royal Quay estate. Bear right then left between a convenience store and the Gallions Hotel **9**, a Grade II listed building, which was where passengers stayed on the eve of embarkation in the days when liners used the Royal Docks. Though no longer a hotel it how has a bar and restaurant. Keep ahead past concrete blocks along a paved footpath and through a gap in a fence to reach Atlantis Avenue **P** *(buses)*, with Gallions Reach DLR Station **Q** almost opposite. The dazzling, windowless orange, red and white building is Armada Point, home of

BDM Logistics and Management. The apparent superfluity of this little-used dual carriageway results from an abandoned plan for it to lead to a new bridge over the Thames.

The next mile of the Capital Ring includes a short stretch of grassy footpath, which can be muddy, and some flights of steps; it also crosses two narrow lock gates with sheer drops into the water, protected by chains. The area is awaiting redevelopment and can seem rather lonely and desolate. *If this is not suitable for you, follow the alternative route by turning left along Atlantis Avenue to cross the Sir Steve Redgrave Bridge **8**, which carries the A112 Woolwich Manor Way and has wonderful views of the docks and aircraft using London City Airport **6**. On its far side, continue along the road until it swings right, where turn left into Fishguard Way **O** and keep ahead through Galleons Point Estate to the riverside promenade **U**, crossing two roads.*

Turn right along Atlantis Avenue to its end, passing a sober, grey complex which houses the London offices of the Swiss company Bühler, specialists in technology for the food industry. Keep ahead on a broad, bonded gravel path past Bawley Court apartments to the Thames riverside **R**, here dominated by the Port of London Authority's radio mast. Looking back, note the four metal 'minarets' at each corner of a 'sewerduct', which takes the NOSE (your companion on Walk 14) over the A112 road. This part of the river is called Gallions Reach **10**, named after the Galyons, a leading family in this area in the 14th century. The word 'reach' in this instance refers to an open stretch of water along a river; originally it indicated the distance that could be sailed by a vessel on one tack. The land on the far bank used to be the Royal Arsenal's weapons testing ground, and much of this is now occupied by the expanding town of Thamesmead. Still on the far bank, the point where the river bends is Tripcock Ness (also known as Margaret Ness); it was here, on 3 September 1878, that the SS *Princess Alice*, a passenger vessel en route from Gravesend to London, collided with the collier *Bywell Castle* and sank in just four minutes, with the loss of nearly 600 souls – still the worst ever disaster on a British waterway.

On this side of the river, the land to your left used to be Beckton Gasworks, and is clearly waiting for some kindly developer to come along and do something with it. Beyond the stubborn iron piers of an old jetty rises the Barking Creek Flood Barrier, seen earlier from The Greenway.

There is no riverside access to the left yet, but it is hoped that an extension of the Thames Path will eventually push on that way. The Capital Ring now follows the narrow, crooked and somewhat shrubby riverside footpath to the right, leading past an Environment Agency impounding culvert and new apartment blocks. Eventually the path angles around a ramp, which you should ignore to pass along a narrow path on its far side to the Gallions Marina Entrance Lock **S**, which you cross with care on top of either set of lock gates. This 72-foot long lock is a pale shadow of the original one that served Royal Albert Dock, which was 800 feet long and 100 feet wide. What is now the marina used to be a holding area for ships awaiting their unloading berth in the main part of the dock.

Follow the access road **11** (Gallions Entrance Road) for 100 yards until it swings right, then cross over with care to

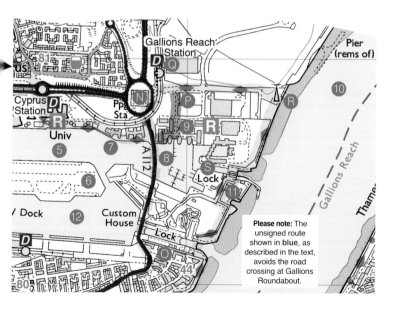

Please note: The unsigned route shown in blue, as described in the text, avoids the road crossing at Gallions Roundabout.

find a narrow, grassy and sometimes muddy footpath between high fences which takes you back to the riverside path. This soon turns inland again and you climb six steps up and eleven down over the flood wall to cross, carefully, the massive gates of the still-functioning lock **T** into King George V Dock **12**, which, like neighbouring Royal Albert, closed to commercial traffic in 1981. This lock has the same dimensions as the original one into the Royal Albert Dock, mentioned above. The largest ship ever to use it (and what an impressive sight it must have been, almost filling the lock) was the 35,655-ton Cunard liner *Mauretania* in 1939, measuring 790 feet long by 88 feet wide – just a whisker to spare on all sides. You may very occasionally have to wait a few minutes while a vessel (sadly no longer of such grand dimensions) is passing into or out of the lock; or you can follow the footpath along this side of the lock to the road and return on the far side.

On the far side of the lock, turn right up steps over the concrete flood wall, then immediately turn sharp left through a gap in the railings and (ignoring the ramp ahead) go back to the riverside, now on the promenade **U** of the Galleons Point Estate – the different spelling apparently the whim of a marketing executive. Follow the promenade to its central point, where the alternative route rejoins the river. There is a food shop over to the right here, in a little shopping centre called Hartlepool Court (all the roads in this estate are named after British ports). On the opposite bank now lie the historic grey-stone buildings of the former Royal Arsenal **13** at Woolwich, established in 1545 – see page 21. The site closed in 1967 and has gradually been handed over for redevelopment. Beyond it rises Shooters Hill, the highest point of the Capital Ring, passed on Walk 1. Floating on the water in front is Royal Arsenal Pier **14**, opened in 2002, served by fast passenger boats from Central London and the occasional sea-going excursion vessel. The land to the left of it used to be the weapons testing area, on which the comparatively new town of Thamesmead is being developed. To the right on the opposite bank, you should just be able to make out journey's end, the little circular red-brick exit of the foot tunnel in Woolwich, less than 1,000 yards away as the crow flies, though still a mile to go for the weary Capital Ring walker.

At the end of the promenade, turn right, go through a gate (press button to open) and turn left down the slope into Bargehouse Road **V**. This is the landing point of an earlier incarnation of the Woolwich Ferry. Bear right on a fenced path along the river wall. Ahead now are the terminals of the Woolwich Free Ferry and the dockyard chimney that you passed on Walk 1. The riverside path

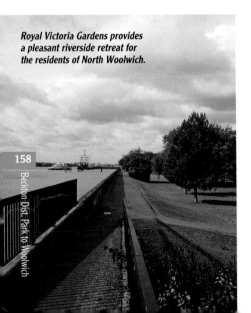

Royal Victoria Gardens provides a pleasant riverside retreat for the residents of North Woolwich.

angles around another former ferry slipway, then climbs to pass through a gate **W** into Royal Victoria Gardens **15**. Continue beside the river, noting on your right a steam hammer of 1888, rescued from a blacksmith's shop in Royal Albert Dock. At the end of the park, keep left up the fenced ramp and go through a gate to continue beside the river wall.

On reaching a derelict jetty **X**, another previous ferry landing point, the route turns right to some steps. Railway enthusiasts may wish to climb these for a view of the former North Woolwich railway station **16** a Grade II listed building, until 2006 the terminus of the North London Line from Richmond via

Stratford. It was replaced by a new branch of the Docklands Light Railway to King George V further north (see Capital Ring link below), which was extended to Woolwich in 2009. The station building and the old sidings had been used as a railway museum and its future is uncertain. Turn left by the steps to continue beside the river wall almost to the ferry terminal, then bear sharp right up a ramp **Y**. Go up and down, then turn sharp right, back along the approach road. Cross with care past the head of the car-ferry queues towards North Woolwich Bus Station, then turn right to the circular red-brick entrance **Z** into the Woolwich Foot Tunnel **17**.

Although the Woolwich Free Ferry (see Walk 1) crosses the river parallel to the tunnel, most Capital Ring walkers will surely eschew the spartan lounges of the ferry to complete their epic journey on foot through the tunnel. However, claustrophobics may prefer the ferry. At the time of writing, the tunnel entrance building was undergoing refurbishment and surrounded by a blue fence, with access through a narrow gap on its near side. There may be short periods when it has to be closed, during which you will have to use the ferry. The Woolwich Foot Tunnel, opened in 1912, is open 24 hours a day and is 550 yards (495 metres) long. Please note that dogs must be kept on a lead.

Although there are lifts at each end, purists may wish to use the steps – 126 down on the north side, 101 up on the south side. Halfway through, you return to the London Borough of Greenwich, which shares responsibility for the tunnel with Newham. You are now at the lowest point of the Capital Ring, around 60 feet (18 metres) below sea level. Having reached the top of the steps on the south side, head for the Capital Ring signpost **AC** and touch it to mark your completion. If there is nobody around, you may even feel inclined to give three cheers.

Congratulations! If you would like a certificate, visit the Walk London website www.walklondon.org.uk, click 'Capital Ring' then scroll down to 'Completion Certificate'.

PART THREE
Useful Information

Transport

It will make good sense for most Capital Ring walkers to use public transport. This offers many advantages, even for motorists. For a start, parking for long periods is difficult or impractical in many areas. You won't need to get back to your car, which may not be easy when the finish of the walk is miles from the start. It also means you can forget about the security of your vehicle, minimise pollution and have a beer or two with no qualms. More information follows, but remember that it is subject to change – always check with the relevant travel information line.

Ticketing in London

The following information was valid at the time of publication but is subject to change at any time.

Pay As You Go/Oyster. By far the easiest and most convenient way to pay for travel in London is to pay as you go, using a contactless payment debit, credit or pre-paid card or mobile device, then you're ready to go! You can pay as you go on all Transport for London (TfL) services and most National Rail services in London (not Heathrow Express services or between Hayes & Harlington and Heathrow on Heathrow Connect services). Just make sure that you touch in at the start and touch out at the end of your journey. On buses and trams, just touch in as you board. The fare charged depends on when you travel and which service you use.

To check the fare before you travel, go to *www.tfl.gov.uk/fares.* For individual journey fares, you should use TfL's single fare finder: *https://tfl.gov.uk/fares-and-payments/fares/single-fare-finder.*

Or you can get an Oyster card and put money on it to pay as you go. It can be bought online (https://oyster.tfl.gov.uk), at stations or tram stops, TfL visitor centres, or many newsagents and other shops.

You can buy a Day Travelcard or a One Day Bus & Tram Pass (see below), but generally Pay As

You Go is better value as you only pay for the journeys you make. When the total cost for all journeys reaches a pre-determined limit, a cap is applied. When you reach a cap, you won't be charged for further journeys in the same zones for the rest of the day. For further information visit *https://tfl.gov.uk/fares-and-payments/contactless/what-is-capping.*

Day Travelcards. These allow you to travel as much as you like, as often as you like for one day. Whether your travel starts before 09.30 on a weekday or after, you can use them on bus, Tube, tram, DLR, London Overground, TfL Rail and most National Rail services within London. Day Travelcards can also be used on the Emirates Air Line and some river services.

One Day Bus & Tram Passes. You can buy a One Day Bus & Tram Pass from Oyster Ticket Stops (newsagents across London) or Tube stations. It gives you unlimited travel on all TfL buses and trams. You may prefer to pay as you go with a contactless payment or Oyster card as you only pay for the journeys you make.

Freedom Passes. If you have a London Freedom Pass, you can use it at any time for any journey operated by TfL (buses, trams, London Underground, London Overground, Docklands Light Railway, TfL Rail). You can use it on local buses that are not operated by TfL but only between 09.30 and 23.00, or any time at weekends and on public holidays. It can be used on National Rail services on Mondays to Fridays between 09.30 and 04.30 the following morning, and at any time at weekends or on public holidays. A Freedom Pass also entitles the holder to a discount on some river services and the Emirates Air Line.

Discounted or free travel. If you have a valid English National Concessionary Travel scheme bus pass, you can use this on all TfL bus and tram services. If you have a Railcard, you can get the Railcard discount set on an Oyster card to get a third off off-peak Pay As You Go travel.

You can get more information at *www.tfl.gov.uk/fares.*

Travel Information

Most transport services in Zones 2, 3 and 4 are reasonably frequent, even on Saturdays and Sundays. However, some services operate less frequently at weekends and in a few cases not at all on Sundays. You are advised to check service details in advance. Details of services and times for all London's public transport services can be obtained from the TfL Journey Planner service, by telephone on 0343 222 1234 or website http://journeyplanner.tfl.gov.uk.

The Starting Points

These are the starting points, all at stations, for each of the 15 walks of the Capital Ring. Each has a frequent service from Central London, usually at least every 30 minutes. There are other options where you can start or finish: at stations, as shown, plus many points in between served by buses. This information is only intended as a guide, and you should check it by calling the travel information services mentioned above.

1 4 **Woolwich Arsenal** (for Foot Tunnel). Docklands Light Railway from Bank and Canary Wharf. South Eastern from Charing Cross, Waterloo East, London Bridge or Cannon Street. Other station with Capital Ring link: Woolwich Dockyard. Riverbus: Royal Arsenal.

2 4 **Falconwood**. South Eastern from Charing Cross, Waterloo East, London Bridge, Cannon Street or Victoria. Other station with Capital Ring link: Mottingham.

3 4 **Grove Park**. South Eastern from Charing Cross, Waterloo East, London Bridge or Cannon Street. Other station passed: Penge East. Other stations with Capital Ring link: Ravensbourne, Kent House, Penge West.

4 3/4 **Crystal Palace**. Southern from London Bridge or Victoria. Other station with Capital Ring link: Streatham.

5 3 **Streatham Common**. Southern from Victoria. Other stations passed: Wandsworth Common, Earlsfield. Other station with Capital Ring link: Balham.

6 3 **Wimbledon Park**. District Line from Central London.

7 4 **Richmond**. District Line from London. South West Trains from Waterloo. London Overground. Other station with Capital Ring link: Brentford.

8 4 **Boston Manor** (for Osterley Lock). Piccadilly Line from Central London. Other station passed: South Greenford. Other station with Capital Ring link: Hanwell (no Sunday service).

9 4 **Greenford**. Central Line from Central London. First Great Western from Paddington. Other stations passed: Sudbury Hill, Sudbury Hill Harrow (Monday–Friday only). Other stations with Capital Ring link: Harrow-on-the-Hill, Northwick Park.

10 4 **South Kenton**. Bakerloo Line from Central London. London Overground from Euston. Other stations passed: Preston Road. Other stations with Capital Ring link: Wembley Park, Hendon, Brent Cross Bus Station.

11 3/4 **Hendon Central** (for Hendon Park). Northern Line from Central London. Other station passed: East Finchley. Note that Hendon Central is in Zone 3 if you are travelling from Zones 1, 2 or 3, but in Zone 4 if travelling from Zones 4, 5 or 6, or from outside Greater London.

12 3 **Highgate**. Northern Line from Central London. Other stations with Capital Ring link: Crouch Hill, Finsbury Park, Manor House.

13 2 **Stoke Newington**. NXEA from Liverpool Street. Other station with Capital Ring link: Clapton.

14 2 **Hackney Wick**. London Overground (change at Stratford or Highbury & Islington for Central London). Other stations with Capital Ring link: Pudding Mill Lane, West Ham.

15 3 **Royal Albert** (for Beckton District Park). Docklands Light Railway from Bank. Other stations passed: Cyprus, Gallions Reach. Other stations with Capital Ring link: King George V, Woolwich Arsenal.

Useful Addresses

British Walking Federation,
5 Windsor Square, Reading RG1 2TH
✎ info@bwf-ivv.org.uk
ⓘ www.bwf-ivv.org.uk. *Through its member clubs, organises non-competitive events and permanent trails for people of all ages and abilities, who receive awards for achievement.*

Canal and River Trust, 500 Elder Gate, Milton Keynes, MK9 1BB
☎ 0303 040 4040
✎ customer.services@canalrivertrust.org.uk
ⓘ www.canalrivertrust.org.uk *Formerly known as British Waterways, manages and cares for 2,000 miles of canals, navigable rivers and docks, including the Grand Union Canal and Lee Navigation.*

City of London (Open Spaces Directorate), Guildhall, PO Box 270, London EC2P 2EJ
☎ 020 7332 3505
✎ openspaces.directorate@ cityoflondon.gov.uk
ⓘ www.cityoflondon.gov.uk. *Owns and manages many open spaces in and near London, including Highgate Woods.*

English Heritage, 1 Waterhouse Square, London EC1N 2ST
☎ 020 7973 3000
✎ customers@english-heritage.org.uk
ⓘ www.english-heritage.org.uk. *Maintains many historic properties including Eltham Palace.*

Greater London Authority, City Hall, The Queen's Walk, Southwark, London SE1 2AA
☎ 020 7983 4000
✎ via website
ⓘ www.london.gov.uk

Lee Valley Park, Information Centre, Myddelton House, Bulls Cross, Enfield EN2 9HG ☎ 03000 030610
✎ info@leevalleypark.org.uk
ⓘ www.leevalleypark.org.uk

Living Streets, 4th Floor, Universal House, 88 Wentworth Street, London E1 7SA
☎ 020 7377 4900
✎ info@living streets.org.uk
ⓘ www.livingstreets. org.uk. *Campaigns for better and safer conditions for all pedestrians.*

London Boroughs. *Responsible for highway and footpath maintenance, and for management of most of the parks along the Capital Ring. Their parks departments can provide details of park closing times, where relevant.*

Barnet. North London Business Park, Oakleigh Road South, London N11 1NP
☎ 020 8359 2000
✎ first.contact@barnet.gov.uk
ⓘ www.barnet.gov.uk

Brent. Brent Civic Centre, Engineers Way, Wembley HA9 0FJ
☎ 020 8937 1234
✎ customer.services@brent .gov.uk
ⓘ www.brent.gov.uk

Bromley. Civic Centre, Stockwell Close, Bromley BR1 3UH
☎ 0300 303 8672
✎ via website
ⓘ www.bromley.gov.uk

Croydon. Bernard Weatherill House, 8 Mint Walk, Croydon CR0 1EA
☎ 020 8726 6000
✎ via website
ⓘ www.croydon.gov.uk

Ealing. Council Offices, Perceval House, 14 Uxbridge Road, Ealing, London W5 2HL
☎ 020 8825 5000
✎ via website
ⓘ www.ealing.gov.uk

Greenwich (Royal Borough of). Town Hall, Wellington Street, Woolwich, London SE18 6HQ
☎ 020 8854 8888
✎ via website
ⓘ www.royalgreenwich.gov.uk

Hackney. Hackney Service Centre, 1 Hillman Street, London E8 1DY
☎ 020 8356 3000
✎ info@hackney.gov.uk
ⓘ www.hackney.gov.uk

Haringey. Civic Centre, High Road, Wood Green, London N22 8LE
☎ 020 8489 0000
✎ via website
ⓘ www.haringey.gov.uk

Harrow. Civic Centre, Station Road, Harrow HA1 2UH
☎ 020 8424 1881
✉ publicrealm@harrow.gov.uk
ⓘ www.harrow.gov.uk

Hounslow. Civic Centre, Lampton Road, Hounslow TW3 4DN
☎ 020 8583 2000
✉ via website
ⓘ www.hounslow.gov.uk

Islington. 222 Upper Street, Islington, London N1 1XR
☎ 020 7527 2000
✉ via website
ⓘ www.islington.gov.uk

Kingston-upon-Thames (Royal Borough of). Guildhall 2, High Street, Kingston KT1 1EU
☎ 020 8547 5000
✉ information@rbk.kingston.gov.uk
ⓘ www.kingston.gov.uk

Lambeth. Town Hall, Brixton Hill, Brixton, London SW2 1RW
☎ 020 7926 1000
✉ infoservice@lambeth.gov.uk
ⓘ www.lambeth.gov.uk

Lewisham. Town Hall, Catford Road, Catford, London SE6 4RU
☎ 020 8314 6000
✉ via website
ⓘ www.lewisham.gov.uk

Merton. Civic Centre, London Road, Morden SM4 5DX
☎ 020 8274 4901
✉ mertonlink@merton.gov.uk
ⓘ www.merton.gov.uk

Newham. Town Hall Annexe, 330 Barking Road, East Ham, London E6 2RT
☎ 020 8430 2000
✉ via website
ⓘ www.newham.gov.uk

Richmond-upon-Thames. Civic Centre, 44 York Street, Twickenham TW1 3BZ
☎ 020 8891 1411
✉ via website
ⓘ www.richmond.gov.uk

Tower Hamlets. Town Hall, Mulberry Place, 5 Clove Crescent, Blackwall, London E14 2BG

☎ 020 7364 5020
✉ via website
ⓘ www.towerhamlets.gov.uk

Waltham Forest. Town Hall, Forest Road, Walthamstow, London E17 4JF
☎ 020 8496 3000
✉ wfdirect@walthamforest.gov.uk
ⓘ www.walthamforest.gov.uk

Wandsworth. Town Hall, Wandsworth High Street, London SW18 2PU
☎ 020 8871 6000
✉ via website
ⓘ www.wandsworth.gov.uk

London Wildlife Trust, Dean Bradley House, 52 Horseferry Road, London SW1P 2AF
☎ 020 7261 0447
✉ via website
ⓘ www.wildlondon.org.uk. *Cares for 57 nature reserves in Greater London, including several along the Capital Ring.*

Long Distance Walkers Association, c/o Bellevue, Princes Street, Ulverston LA12 7NB
✉ membership@ldwa.org.uk
ⓘ www.ldwa.org.uk. *Represents interests of long-distance walkers and organises walks through a network of groups, including one for London.*

Open Spaces Society, 25a Bell Street, Henley-on-Thames RG9 2BA
☎ 01491 573535
✉ office1@oss.org.uk
ⓘ www.oss.org.uk. *Protects common land, greens and open spaces.*

Ordnance Survey, Adanac Drive, Southampton SO16 0AS
☎ 03456 050505
✉ via website
ⓘ customerservices@os.uk. *Publishes maps covering the whole of the United Kingdom.*

Thames Clippers, 61 Trinity Buoy Wharf, London E14 0FP
✉ via website
ⓘ www.thamesclippers.com. *For information about fast river services between Central London, Putney and Woolwich.*

Thames River Services, Westminster Pier, Victoria Embankment, London SW1A 2JH
☎ 020 7930 4097
✔ via website
ⓘ www.thamesriverservices.co.uk.
For information about services on the Thames between Central London, Greenwich, Thames Barrier and Richmond.

The Ramblers, 2nd Floor, Camelford House, 87 Albert Embankment, Vauxhall, London SE1 7TW
☎ 020 7339 8500
✔ ramblers@ramblers.org.uk
ⓘ www.ramblers.org.uk. *Takes up path problems and organises walks through a network of local groups, including 20 covering Greater London.*

Transport for London (TfL), Customer Services, 4th Floor, 14 Pier Walk, North Greenwich, London SE10 0ES
☎ 020 7222 5600
✔ walking@tfl.gov.uk
ⓘ www.tfl.gov.uk/walking
Promotes and provides information about London's top seven walking routes.

Tourist Information Centres *can offer help with local accommodation, transport and details of places to visit:*

Central London. 1 Lower Regent Street, London SW1Y 4XT (personal callers only)
ⓘ www.visitlondon.com

City of London Tourist Information Centre. St Paul's Churchyard, City of London EC4M 8BX *(personal callers only)*

Greenwich. Pepys House, 2 Cutty Sark Gardens, Greenwich, London SE10 9LW
☎ 0870 608 2000
✔ tic@greenwich.gov.uk
ⓘ www.visitgreenwich.org.uk

Kingston. Visit Kingston, Neville House, 3rd Floor, 55 Eden Street, Kingston upon Thames KT1 1BW
☎ 020 8547 1221
✔ via website
ⓘ www.kingstonfirst.co.uk

Lewisham. Lewisham Library, 199 Lewisham High Street, London SE13 6LG
☎ 020 8297 8317

Richmond. Civic Centre, 44 York Street, Twickenham TW1 3BZ
☎ 020 8891 1411
✔ info@visitrichmond.co.uk
ⓘ www.visitrichmond.co.uk

Ordnance Survey Maps Covering The Capital Ring

Landranger Maps (scale 1:50 000): 176 West London area and 177 East London area.

Explorer Maps (scale 1:25 000): 162 Greenwich & Gravesend, 161 London South, 173 London North. Parts of Walks 12 and 13 also appear on 174 Epping Forest & Lea Valley, but this duplicates the sections included on sheet 162.

OS Custom Made Maps. It is possible to buy a special Ordnance Survey map in the Landranger style (1:50 000 scale) covering the whole Capital Ring, using the 'OS Custom Made' service from their website www.ordnancesurvey.co.uk/shop. Click on Custom Made maps, then under 'Choose the centre of your map' type W1A 1AA, click the Landranger option and follow the instructions. It is suggested that you put 'Capital Ring' as the main title and '78 mile trail around London' as the sub-title. The route is marked by the standard OS lozenge symbol for walking routes. Although Select maps are also available in the Explorer style (1:25 000 scale), you would need two maps to cover the whole route.

The Official Guides to all c

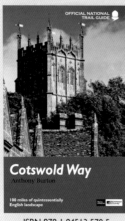

Cotswold Way
Anthony Burton

100 miles of quintessentially
English landscape

ISBN 978 1 84513 570 5

Cleveland Way
Ian Sampson

Over 100 miles of magnificent
walking on the North York Moors

ISBN 978 1 84513 781 6

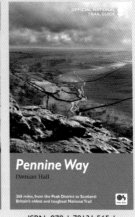

Pennine Way
Damian Hall

268 miles, from the Peak District to Scotland:
Britain's oldest and toughest National Trail

ISBN 978 1 78131 565 1

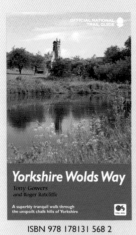

Yorkshire Wolds Way
Tony Gowers
and Roger Ratcliffe

A superbly tranquil walk through
the unspoilt chalk hills of Yorkshire

ISBN 978 178131 568 2

**Pembrokeshire
Coast Path**
Wales Coast Path: St Dogmaels to Amroth
Brian John

ISBN 978 1 84513 782 3

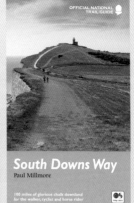

South Downs Way
Paul Millmore

100 miles of glorious chalk downland
for the walker, cyclist and horse rider

ISBN 978 1 78131 563 7

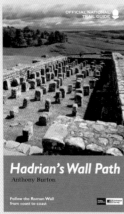

Hadrian's Wall Path
Anthony Burton

Follow the Roman Wall
from coast to coast

ISBN 978 1 84513 808 0

The Ridgeway
Anthony Burton

87 miles of downland walking
from Wiltshire to the Chilterns

ISBN 978 178131 063 2

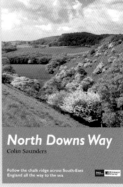

North Downs Way
Colin Saunders

Follow the chalk ridge across South-East
England all the way to the sea

ISBN 978 178131 500 2

ritain's National Trails

Thames Path
in the Country
David Sharp and Tony Gowers
From the source to Hampton Court

ISBN 978 1 84513 717 5

Thames Path
in London
Phoebe Clapham
From Hampton Court to Crayford Ness:
50 miles of historic riverside walk

ISBN 978 1 78131 574 3

Peddars Way and
Norfolk Coast Path
Bruce Robinson
with Mike Robinson and Tim Lidstone-Scott
92 miles from the Brecks to
salt marsh and sea cliffs

ISBN 978 1 78131 566 8

South West Coast Path
Minehead to Padstow
Roland Tarr
160 miles of coastal walking from
Exmoor to North Cornwall

ISBN 978 178131 564 4

South West Coast Path
Padstow to Falmouth
John Macadam
From golden beaches to rugged coves
around Britain's southernmost tip

ISBN 978 178131 062 5

Offa's Dyke Path
Ernie and Kathy Kay and Mark Richards
Edited by Tony Gowers
Follow the ancient earthwork for 177 miles
from the Severn Estuary to the Irish Sea

ISBN 978 1 78131 066 3

South West Coast Path
Falmouth to Exmouth
Brian Le Messurier
172 miles of dramatic coves, cliffs and
beaches from Cornwall to Devon

ISBN 978 1 78131 486 9

South West Coast Path
Exmouth to Poole
Roland Tarr
From Jane Austen's Cobb to Lulworth Cove
– over 100 miles of historic coastline

ISBN 978 178131 567 5

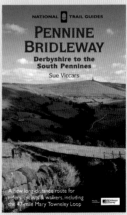

NATIONAL TRAIL GUIDES
PENNINE BRIDLEWAY
Derbyshire to the South Pennines
Sue Viccars

A new long-distance route for
riders, cyclists & walkers, including
the 47-mile Mary Towneley Loop

ISBN 1 85410 957 X

Other guide books from Aurum Press

The Capital Ring
Colin Saunders

78 miles of green corridor encircling inner London

ISBN 978 1 78131 569 9

The London Loop
David Sharp with Colin Saunders

140 miles of secret countryside to walk in a green corridor around London

ISBN 978 1 84513 787 8

West Highland Way
Anthony Burton

94 miles of Scottish moor and mountain in Britain's most spectacular long-distance walk

ISBN 978 178131 089 2

The Coast to Coast Walk
Martin Wainwright

The classic high-level walk from Irish Sea to North Sea

ISBN 978 1 84513 560 6

Northumberland Coast Path
Roland Tarr

From the centre of Newcastle to the Scottish border

ISBN 978 178131 562 0

Wales Coast Path
Tenby to Swansea
Chris Moss

Endless sandy beaches and the beautiful Gower Peninsula

ISBN 978 178131 067 0

Somerset Coast Path
Damian Hall

121 miles of beautiful scenery, history and surprises

ISBN 978 1 78131 185 1

Camino de Santiago
Sergi Ramis

The ancient Way of Saint James pilgrimage route from the French Pyrenees to Santiago de Compostela

ISBN 978 1 78131 223 0

CAROLINE DALE
SKYLINE LONDON
A GUIDE TO THE FINEST VIEWS FROM THE CAPITAL'S HIGH POINTS

ISBN 978 1 84513 762 5